FREEDOM FROM ADDICTION

WORKBOOK

NEIL T. ANDERSON
AND MIKE & JULIA QUARLES

Gospel Light

Gospel Light is an evangelical Christian publisher dedicated to serving the local church. We believe God's vision for Gospel Light is to provide church leaders with biblical, user-friendly materials that will help them evangelize, disciple and minister to children, youth and families.

We hope this Gospel Light resource will help you discover biblical truth for your own life and help you minister to adults. God bless you in your work.

For a free catalog of resources from Gospel Light please contact your Christian supplier or call 1-800-4-GOSPEL.

PUBLISHING STAFF
William T. Greig, Publisher
Dr. Elmer L. Towns, Senior Consulting Publisher
Dr. Gary S. Greig, Senior Consulting Editor
Jill Honodel, Editor
Pam Weston, Assistant Editor
Kyle Duncan, Associate Publisher
Bayard Taylor, M.Div., Editor, Theological and Biblical Issues
Debi Thayer, Designer

Contents

Introduction

We would like to extend to you our hope for your complete recovery and freedom in Jesus Christ. We believe that He is the answer for every unresolved personal and spiritual conflict in your life. We also believe that the Holy Spirit is the Spirit of truth and He will lead you into all truth which will set you free in Christ. Jesus said, "You will know the truth, and the truth will set you free" (John 8:32, *NIV*). Our evidence is that we have personally experienced that same freedom and have helped thousands of others discover the truth that they are new creations in Christ who can be set free from their pasts and their addictive behaviors.

The reason we can be so confident is because we have a great God who loves us and is infinitely more powerful than all the collective problems of the universe. We have learned like Paul to put no confidence in the flesh (see Philippians 3:3) nor in any other mortal or man-made program. You will discover that brokenness and dependence upon God are the keys to victory, and that self-sufficiency is the road to destruction. Only when we come to the end of our own resources do we discover God's resources. Paul said, "Not that we are adequate in ourselves to consider anything as coming from ourselves, but our adequacy is from God, who also made us adequate as servants of a new covenant, not of the letter, but of the Spirit; for the letter kills, but the Spirit gives life" (2 Corinthians 3:5,6).

God loves you! That can sound so trite and can be nothing more than shallow and hollow words unless you realize that the love of God is not dependent upon the object of love. God loves us because God is love (see 1 John 4:16). It is His nature to love us whether we perform well or not. "God demonstrates His own love toward us, in that while we were yet sinners [alcoholics, sex addicts, junkies, anorexics, gamblers, kleptomaniacs—in fact, like all of humanity], Christ died for us" (Romans 5:8). He loves us so much that He sacrificed His only begotten Son in order that we could be forgiven of all our sins. Then He adopted us as His own children and gave us eternal life which every Christian receives the moment he or she is born again. We also have

His assurance that He will never leave us or forsake us. You have to choose to believe that even when your emotions and troubled thoughts are screaming otherwise. Jesus is *the* Bondage Breaker and He came to set captives free. He is the only one who can. That is the most important belief that must penetrate your heart and be owned by every person struggling with addictive behaviors.

The second most important belief is knowing who you are in Christ. No person can consistently behave in a way that is inconsistent with how he or she perceives him- or herself. It is not what you do that determines who you are; it is who you are and how you perceive yourself that determines what you do. We choose to believe the words of the apostle Paul when he said, "Therefore from now on we recognize no man according to the flesh" (2 Corinthians 5:16). Paul never identifies Christians by who they were in Adam. Instead he identifies them by who they are in Christ. Every struggling Christian has patterns of the flesh (the old nature) that reveal how he or she learned to cope, succeed or merely survive independent from God. All of us have to learn how to identify and then renounce those patterns of the flesh in order to live like the children of God we really are. First John 3:1-3 clearly states:

> See how great a love the Father has bestowed upon us, that we should be called children of God; and such we are. For this reason the world does not know us, because it did not know Him. Beloved, now we are children of God, and it has not appeared as yet what we shall be. We know that, when He appears, we shall be like Him, because we will see Him just as He is. And everyone who has this hope fixed on Him purifies himself, just as He is pure.

The Goal

The goal of this study is to help you become free in Christ and more like Him in character. Paul said, "We proclaim Him, admonishing every man and teaching every man with all wisdom, that we may present every man complete in Christ" (Colossians 1:28).

We believe that abstinence from addictive behavior is an incomplete goal. We don't abstain in order to get right with God, we get right with God in order to abstain. We don't keep the law in order to have a right relationship with God, we enter into a right relationship with God in order to keep the law. People who struggle with addictions are no different from any other needy person. We all need to be loved, accepted and affirmed as children of God, and only Christ can meet all our

needs according to His riches in glory (see Ephesians 1:18). If abstinence were the goal, then Ephesians 5:18 would read, "Do not get
drunk with wine, but abstain!" But thankfully it says that we must "be
filled with the Spirit" rather than "abstain." Paul expressed this vital
truth when he wrote, "I say, walk by the Spirit, and you will not carry
out the desire of the flesh" (Galatians 5:16).

All participants in the *Freedom from Addiction Workbook* should first
process the Steps to Freedom in Christ. *The Steps to Freedom in Christ*
(STFIC) can be purchased through your local Christian bookstore or
from the Freedom in Christ Ministries office. They are also included in
the appendix of *Freedom from Addiction* which is the companion text for
this workbook. The STFIC is a comprehensive repentance process of
submitting to God and resisting the devil (see James 4:7). People all
over the world are resolving their personal and spiritual conflicts and
finding their freedom in Christ by using this discipleship and counseling tool. The theology and practical uses of the STFIC are given in
the book *Helping Others Find Freedom in Christ.*

We estimate that about 85 percent of the Christian population can
process the STFIC on their own. The chances of that happening are
greatly increased if they would first read *Victory over the Darkness* and
The Bondage Breaker. Both books have inductive studies and corresponding video series which can be obtained from the Freedom in
Christ Ministries office, 491 East Lambert Road, La Habra, CA, 90631,
telephone number (562) 691-9128. If you are struggling with an addiction, you may need someone to help walk you through the STFIC.

At a very minimum, each participant must go through the Steps to
Freedom in Christ either on his or her own or with the help of a
trained Christian encourager before beginning this workbook. The
effectiveness of the *Freedom from Addiction Workbook* will also be greatly enhanced if you take from 16 to 24 weeks to process the material. Do
not hurry through each chapter thinking you must finish a chapter a
week. It took a period of time for your addiction to develop and it will
take time to become free from that addiction. Remember "that He who
began a good work in you will perfect it until the day of Christ Jesus"
(Philippians 1:6).

Personal Responsibility

It must be stated that the steps themselves do not set you free. The one who sets you free is Christ, and what sets you free is your response to Him through repentance and faith. We are all victims of a fallen society, but whether we remain victims is our choice. Christ has done all He needs to do for you to live a free and productive life. He paid the penalty for your sin, forgave your debt and defeated the devil. He gave you eternal life, provided the Word of God which is the truth and placed His Holy Spirit within you to bear witness in your spirit that you are a child of God and guide you into the truth that will set you free.

Nobody is born with addictive behaviors, but we are all born dead in our trespasses and sins (see Ephesians 2:1). We had neither the presence of God in our lives nor the knowledge of His ways. Consequently we all learned to live our lives independent from God. Even when we were born again and became new creations in Christ, nobody pushed the erase button to clear the computer we call our mind. That is why Paul said, "Do not be conformed to this world, but be transformed by the renewing of your mind, that you may prove what the will of God is, that which is good and acceptable and perfect" (Romans 12:2).

Assume the responsibility to appropriate the freedom that Christ purchased for you on the cross. No one else can do that for you. Freedom in Christ must come first. Once you have resolved all the personal and spiritual conflicts that keep you bound to the past and the sin that so easily entangles you, then you will experience the freedom to be all that God calls you to be. No one can become a Christian without admitting he or she is sinful by nature and separated from God. We must all throw ourselves upon the mercy of God and call upon His name in order to be saved. In a similar vein we must admit to our own sinful addictions and stop living a lie before we can experience the freedom that God wants us all to have. You will not be helped by this workbook and the companion text unless you are willing to speak the truth in love and walk in the light as He is in the light. Then and only then can we have fellowship one with one another (see 1 John 1:5-9). Denial and cover-up only contribute to addiction. We are as sick as we are secretive, and we are as defeated as we are in denial.

Accountability Encouragers

We absolutely need God, and we necessarily need each other. We were not created to live our lives alone. Accountability begins with God. The thoughts and intentions of our hearts and everything we have ever done or said is known by Him (see Hebrews 4:12,13). So why not be honest with Him? His unconditional love and acceptance of us is beyond question. God is not out to get us. He is out to restore us. Thinking we can hide from Him is pure deception.

In addition to being honest and open with God, everybody should have at least one person that he or she can be totally open and honest with. A good support group can provide some helpful accountability, but the degree of intimacy and accountability is inversely proportional to the size of the group. We recommend that recovery ministries use this workbook as a group study, but each member of the group should have at least one other person to be mutually accountable with. Consider the following four words and ask yourself, *From which end of the list does God approach us?*

> Authority
> Accountability
> Affirmation
> Acceptance

Surely there is a need for accountability, but the authority figure who demands accountability without acceptance and affirmation will never get it. When people are accepted and affirmed, they will voluntarily be accountable to the authority figure. Even though God is the ultimate authority in the universe, He has offered us a ministry of reconciliation based on affirmation and acceptance. No words of Jesus were ever recorded that said in effect, "Listen, you sick and sinful creatures, shape up because I am your Creator God!" On the contrary, sinners loved to be around Jesus, and He waged war against the hypocrites. The same should be true of any ministry of reconciliation and recovery.

On the other hand, encouragers should care enough to confront. A person is in trouble when he or she starts to miss meetings or appointments. Excuses, rationalizations, broken promises and cover-ups need to be confronted immediately. Most people don't fall off the wagon because of a lack of knowledge or even a lack of desire. They fail for lack of follow-through. Knowing that you will have to share openly with a trusted encourager, and being held lovingly accountable is what keeps most people on track.

Make a commitment now to be totally honest and accountable to your encourager. Not telling your encourager that you slipped and fell is worse than slipping and falling. Living a lie and walking in darkness are characteristics of the kingdom of darkness, and you will find yourself subject to the god of this world. Speaking the truth in love with your encourager (see Ephesians 4:25) and walking in the light (see 1 John 1:5-10) are the two biggest tickets to maintaining your freedom in Christ.

Ministry Strategies

The ideal strategy is to resolve personal and spiritual conflicts first. This can be accomplished by reading *Victory over the Darkness* and *The Bondage Breaker* and going through the Steps to Freedom in Christ. The same material is covered in the video/audio series *Resolving Personal and Spiritual Conflicts* available from Freedom in Christ Ministries. The curriculum for teaching the same material is called *Breaking Through to Spiritual Maturity*. At a minimum, each person needs to go through the Steps to Freedom in Christ first, either alone, with a trusted encourager or with the group. If you purchased the *Freedom from Addiction Video Study* along with this workbook, the second video will walk you through *The Steps to Freedom in Christ* booklet. Think of the STFIC as a comprehensive process of detoxing the soul. Just as some alcoholics and addicts need to detox their bodies, *every* child of God needs to go through a fierce moral inventory and repent in order to purify his or her soul. Listen to the cry of David's heart in Psalm 32:1-7 after months of covering up his sin with Bathsheba:

> How blessed is he whose transgression is forgiven, whose sin is covered! How blessed is the man to whom the LORD does not impute iniquity, and in whose spirit there is no deceit!
>
> When I kept silent about my sin, my body wasted away through my groaning all day long. For day and night Thy hand was heavy upon me; my vitality was drained away as with the fever heat of summer.
>
> I acknowledged my sin to Thee, and my iniquity I did not hide; I said, "I will confess my transgressions to the LORD"; and Thou didst forgive the guilt of my sin.
>
> Therefore, let everyone who is godly pray to Thee in a time when Thou mayest be found; surely in a flood of great waters they shall not reach him. Thou art my hiding place; thou doest preserve me from trouble; Thou doest surround me with songs of deliverance.

Nobody likes to share intimate details about their lives just for the purpose of sharing. But we have discovered that in the context of acceptance, affirmation and confidentiality people are more than willing to share even shameful issues in their lives for the purpose of resolving their problems. Paul expresses this vital truth in 2 Corinthians 7:9,10:

> I now rejoice, not that you were made sorrowful, but that you were made sorrowful to the point of repentance; for you were made sorrowful according to the will of God, in order that you might not suffer loss in anything through us. For the sorrow that is according to the will of God produces a repentance without regret, leading to salvation.

We have never seen anyone come under the conviction of sin, totally repent and regret it afterwards. They are relieved as David was because it is finally over with. Freedom and forgiveness is what they sense. Living in fear of being exposed and living a lie is worse than getting caught. People feel a sense of relief when they finally acknowledge their sin, even though they have to face their consequences.

How to Use This Workbook

There is no time limit for processing this workbook. You can't move any faster than you can educate. The goal is not to get through the material in a certain amount of time, nor is it to master the material. The goal is to let the truth of God enter your heart so as to master you in order to be free in Christ. The first nine chapters of the workbook have corresponding chapters to be read in *Freedom from Addiction*. The assigned chapters should be read before completing the exercises in this workbook. For each chapter in this workbook there are seven sections:

A. **Understanding the Problem:** The subject matter and the problem it presents to those in bondage is introduced, emphasizing the lie that is commonly believed and accepted.

B. **Making a Personal Appraisal:** Discover the deceptions and blind spots in your belief system. This exercise enables you to see the lies you have believed on this particular subject that keep you in bondage. There will be questions to guide you to see how your past experiences have affected you and your beliefs, then the exposed lie is stated.

C. **Discovering the Truth That Sets You Free:** The Bible study enables you to discover the truth that sets you free.

D. **Stating the Truth:** The truth is clearly stated and you are encouraged to write out any other truths you have personally learned from studying Scripture.

E. **Illustrating the Truth:** You will be encouraged to respond to illustrations taken from *Freedom from Addiction*.

F. **Appropriating the Truth:** You will make a list of the lies you need to renounce and the corresponding truth you need to announce based on what you have learned in personal study, as well as insights you have gotten from the group interaction.

G. **Personalizing the Truth:** Finally you will be encouraged to personalize Scripture and write out statements of truth.

Weekly Meetings

The exercises in this workbook should be completed before the weekly meetings. A willingness to complete the exercises, do the corresponding reading in *Freedom from Addiction* and faithful weekly attendance with your group as well as your church are major factors in maintaining your freedom and complete recovery in Christ.

In more extreme cases of addiction, you may be advised to attend a group meeting once a day. That may be necessary for those who need a greater degree of accountability. Some of these meetings may not be Christian or in total agreement with what you will be learning in this study. In such cases we strongly suggest that you choose an accountability encourager who is committed to the truth of God's Word.

The conduct of the weekly meetings is drawn from 1 Peter 4:7-11:

> The end of all things is at hand; therefore, be of sound judgment and sober spirit for the purpose of prayer. Above all, keep fervent in your love for one another, because love covers a multitude of sins. Be hospitable to one another without complaint. As each one has received a special gift, employ it in serving one another as good stewards of the manifold grace of God. Whoever speaks, let him speak, as it were, the utterances of God; whoever serves, let him do so as by the strength which God supplies; so that in all things God may be glorified through Jesus Christ, to whom belongs the glory and dominion forever and ever. Amen.

Using the above passage as a guideline, we recommend that every meeting include a time of introduction and sharing followed by prayer. We suggest that you introduce yourself by saying, "Hi, I'm (name), I'm a child of God (if you are indeed a born-again child of God) and I have struggled with (state the nature of your addiction or bondage)." The group should then respond by saying, "Hi, (name)." After introductions are completed, each group member should share how his or her previous week has gone and any particular needs that he or she has. The rest of the group should then pray for each person's needs.

The group *must be* committed to loving one another, meeting one another's needs and sharing how their needs are being met in Christ. We strongly suggest that each member of the group read *Living Free in Christ* which shows how Christ meets our most critical "being" needs of life, identity, acceptance, security and significance.

This is a ministry of reconciliation (see 2 Corinthians 5:18-21), not condemnation, for "there is therefore now no condemnation for those who are in Christ Jesus" (Romans 8:1). On the other hand, it is consistent with the love of God to confront others if their behavior is counterproductive to their recovery in Christ. You are not counting their sin against them if you point out that what they are believing or doing is damaging their relationship with God and others. Just make sure that you share the truth in love, demonstrating that you have their best interests at heart.

During the group meetings, discussions should be on the material in the workbook centering on the person of Christ and the Word of God. This will include a lot of sharing from personal lives as well as insights into Scripture. Each member should contribute because everyone will benefit from one another's perspectives and giftedness. Sharing should, however, be prompted by the Holy Spirit, not the flesh. The group leader has the responsibility of ensuring that no one dominates the discussion and keeping the meetings focused on Christ and His Word.

Each chapter begins with one of the ten statements of "The Overcomer's Covenant in Christ." You may want to begin each meeting by reading the complete "Overcomer's Covenant in Christ" on page 204 and close each meeting by reading the list affirming who you are "In Christ" on page 205.

About the Video Study

The *Freedom from Addiction Video Study* is a complete package of resources providing a systematic approach to breaking the bondage of addictions. The package includes two videos, one copy of *Freedom from Addiction*, one copy of the *Freedom from Addiction Workbook* and six copies of *The Steps to Freedom in Christ* booklet.

The first video contains 10 brief presentations by Neil Anderson with Mike and Julia Quarles, introducing the workbook activities and encouraging group interaction. The second video features Neil leading individuals through *The Steps to Freedom in Christ* booklet to be used with the accompanying booklets in the video study package. More STFIC booklets are available from your local Christian bookstore or from the Freedom in Christ Ministries office; 491 East Lambert Road, La Habra, CA, 90631; telephone number (562) 691-9128.

Guidelines for Support Groups

The Purpose:

To build a nonjudgmental fellowship base for support where each member is accepted and affirmed for who he or she is so that they may be firmly rooted and built up in Christ in order to live a free and productive life in the power of the Holy Spirit.

The Objectives:

1. To love one another (see 1 John 4:11).
2. To accept one another as Christ has accepted us (see Romans 15:7).
3. To affirm one another according to who we are in Christ (see 1 John 3:1-3).
4. To encourage one another to walk by faith (see 2 Corinthians 5:7,8).
5. To speak the truth in love as members of one another (see Ephesians 4:25).
6. To walk in the light as He is in the light in order to have fellowship with one another (see 1 John 1:5-9).
7. To pray for one another (see Ephesians 6:18).
8. To establish trust and confidentiality (see Proverbs 20:6; 2 Timothy 2:2).
9. To stand together against the father of lies (see John 8:44; 1 Timothy 4:1).
10. To care enough to confront one another in love (see Matthew 18:15).

Some Cautions:

1. Don't play the role of the Holy Spirit in another person's life. It is not our ministry to change one another. Our ministry is for reconciliation with God who has the power to change anyone (see 2 Corinthians 5:17-21).
2. Don't focus on the problem; focus on the solution (see Hebrews 12:2,3). This is not a secular therapy group that helps people cope with their problems or become comfortable with their sin. The goal is to resolve personal and spiritual conflicts in order to be free in Christ.

Reading Assignment: Chapter 1 in *Freedom from Addiction*

How You Got Where You Are

The Overcomer's Covenant in Christ

Statement One

> *I place all my trust and confidence in the Lord, and I put no confidence in the flesh. I declare myself to be dependent upon God. I know that I cannot save myself, nor set myself free by my own efforts and resources. I know that apart from Christ I can do nothing (see John 15:5). I know that all temptation is an attempt to get me to live my life independent from God, but God has provided a way of escape from sin (see 1 Corinthians 10:13).*

Programs, ministries and strategies do not save us nor do they set us free. The one who saves us and sets us free is Christ, and what saves us and sets us free is our response to Him in repentance and faith. This faith is based on the truth of God's Word and the finished work of Christ. The Lord does work through biblically-based ministries that are alive in Christ and committed to the truth that sets people free. We wholeheartedly recommend, support and encourage every overcomer to be a part of a redemptive fellowship under the New Testament covenant of grace. But working a program and depending on a group will not save us nor set us free in Christ even with the best of intentions. Such programs and groups can be very caring and may result in abstinence from alcohol and drugs; but ultimately salvation and freedom can only come from Christ.

The Lord never created humanity to live independent from Him. Adam's sin was an act of rebellion against God, and the result was a severed relationship with Him. Jesus modeled a life totally dependent upon His heavenly Father. Without Christ we are not simply handicapped or less effective; without Christ we can do nothing.

The basis for temptation lies in our desire to meet legitimate needs which only Christ can meet. Sources of our addictions are only the objects of our temptation. To believe that we need them to be somebody, succeed or even survive is to believe a lie. We need Christ because only He can meet all our needs according to His riches in glory.

········· A. Understanding the Problem

Is freedom from addiction really possible? A look at the vast amount of literature on addiction gives us little hope that freedom is possible. Why is this? We need to look no further than ourselves. Almost without exception, those of us who have struggled with addiction have given up on finding freedom and would settle for a way to cope. Alcoholics Anonymous (AA) continues to be the most widely accepted and recommended treatment of choice, but the statistics are not very encouraging. The latest figures indicate that 29 percent of AA members have been sober for more than five years. This is an impressive fact until one considers that approximately one-third of all alcohol abusers improve over time without any treatment, according to William Playfair.[1]

I (Mike) was hopelessly in bondage to alcohol for over five years. When I first began struggling with my addiction, I had been a Christian for 10 years. I was a seminary graduate and an ordained minister. I didn't want to be in bondage and desperately wanted to be free. I tried everything that I knew and everything anybody told me to do, but none of it worked. I got to the point where I had given up on being a good Christian. I had long since given up on the idea of being a productive Christian. I would have gladly settled for just being normal although I wasn't sure what that was. If God had said to me, "I'll make a deal with you, I'll let you be a decent human being and live a sober life" I would have done it in a heartbeat. I had tried everything I knew.

As we look at all the secular treatment programs and resources available, we can only conclude that the world has done a better job in addressing the problem of addiction than the Church has. But neither AA nor any of the myriad of other programs available offer any promise of freedom from addiction. The disease model that the secular world offered left me struggling and coping at best and death or institutionalization at worst. I attended hundreds of AA meetings and went through a secular treatment center with no lasting sense of victory. What I heard was "If you don't deal with the problem, these are the disastrous results you will experience." It seemed like the chief motivation was fear. Stop drinking or suffer the consequences.

Of course there is some truth to that, but if you carry the same logic into Christianity it would sound like this: "Stop sinning or you will go to hell," or "If you do something bad, God will punish you." With this approach a person's whole orientation toward God becomes one of avoiding hell or punishment. Such people live in fear that the hammer of God's wrath will fall on them if they do something wrong. Dear

Christian, the hammer has already fallen. It fell on Christ. He died once for all your sins: past, present and future. "There is no fear in love; but perfect love casts out fear, because fear involves punishment" (1 John 4:18). We are not sinners in the hands of an angry God. We are saints in the hands of a loving God. The true message is "Get right with God so that you can stop sinning and enjoy your relationship with your loving heavenly Father."

It should come as no surprise that the only solution the world can offer is self-improvement, or rather flesh-improvement. In other words, it offers a way to cope, but not change; it offers restraints, but no freedom. Without the gospel there is no freedom from our past. As new creations in Christ we are no longer simply products of our past, we are products of the work of Christ on the cross.

The Christian Approach

Many Christian groups have adopted or Christianized the Twelve Step Program and many others have accepted the disease model. What's wrong with the Twelve Steps? Absolutely nothing. By and large their purpose is accomplished by enabling a person to cope with his or her addiction, and many have been helped to abstain. That is commendable. In addition, many people have found Christ and are coping much better with life as a result of participating with a Christian group that is using the Twelve Step Program.

It is not what the Christian-based Twelve Step Programs are doing that we are concerned about, it is what many are not saying or doing. Unless they have been supplemented with additional biblical material, the Twelve Steps are not sufficient to set a person free from addiction. To be complete they would have to include the following minimum requirements:

1. The personal presence of Christ in our lives
2. The work of Christ on the cross for our sins
3. The forgiveness of our sins and the ability to forgive others
4. A new identity in Christ as children of God
5. The grace of God which frees us from the law
6. Faith, not works, as the means of our salvation and deliverance
7. God's unconditional love and acceptance
8. An understanding of how to walk by the Spirit
9. An answer for guilt and condemnation
10. The knowledge of how to win the battle for the mind

11. Our position in Christ, giving us authority over Satan
12. Our co-crucifixion with Christ which frees us from sin
13. God's grace, not the law, freeing us from the performance-based life and acceptance
14. Our crucifixion to the world, freeing us from the demands of others
15. Spirit-filled prayer for one another
16. The centrality of the Word of God which is the only truth that will set us free
17. An understanding of spiritual warfare

No program can set us free, not even the one we are offering you. Only God can free you. If your goal is to simply stop your addictive behavior, a twelve step program will be beneficial. But God wants you to be alive and free in Christ. True freedom is more than just substituting one addictive behavior for another. It is allowing God to change your thinking about yourself and your behavior. It is truly being transformed by Christ.

If you are actively involved in a twelve step program, that is perfectly okay. There are many fine things that they do, and their years of experience will provide insight into the nature of addiction and co-dependency. It may be beneficial for some to continue in both programs, and use this one to focus on Christ and your relationship with Him.

Have We Bought a Lie?

I (Mike) struggled with alcoholism for over five years. The disease concept is widely accepted in practically every secular program as well as in many Christian programs. The disease concept assumes "once an alcoholic always an alcoholic." But I wanted to be free, and I sought freedom with all my strength. Yet I was always confronted with overwhelming evidence that freedom was not possible. Everyone who knew anything about addiction told me I would have to accept the fact that addiction was something that I would have to fight for the rest of my life and the sooner I accepted that fact the better off I would be. What was this truth that I needed to accept? Simply that I *was* an addict who could not change. Even the godly, mature Christians I knew could offer me no hope. They seemed to accept that addiction was outside the range of God's delivering power or at least their knowledge of it.

Finally, even I could no longer hold out against such sizable evidence. I never will forget the day I believed the lie. It was one of the worst days of my life and I had not even been drinking. I was just driving my car lamenting over the conclusive evidence that no matter how hard I tried and no matter what I did, I could not stop drinking and destroying everything that was good in my life. And then the thought came crashing through that shook me to the very depths of my soul: *It's true, I am a helpless alcoholic. It's hopeless and I'm never going to change.* I had bought the lie that I could never change. As long as I believed the lie, I would remain in bondage.

B. Making a Personal Appraisal

Write out your story below (or on a separate piece of paper) describing how you got to where you are now. Begin as early in your life as you can remember up to your present addictive problem. This is a rough overview of your life. Include childhood experiences, important relationships, education, jobs and career, and any traumas in your life. Also include in broad sketches your involvement with the object of your addiction. Be prepared to share your story with the group.

How Did Your Addiction Begin?

When was the first time you experienced the behavior which led to your addiction? Describe the situation.

Who was there?

What was the occasion?

How did you feel about yourself at the time?

What need did you think it would meet?

Why did it become such a big part of your life?

What did it do for you that nothing else could do?

Can you identify the deception—the lies you believed—that began your path to addiction?

Concerning Your Spiritual Life:

When did you become a Christian?

How did your conversion occur? Describe the sequence of events leading up to it and what you did to become a Christian.

Do you know for sure where you will spend eternity? How do you know?

If you died and appeared before God and He asked you, "Why should I let you into heaven?" what would you say?

Have you ever made a total commitment of your life to God and given Him permission to do anything He wants to do with you? If not, what is keeping you from making such a commitment?

Describe your biggest setbacks, failures, disappointments, tragedy (i.e. loss of job, marital problems, financial problems, humiliating situations, failure to perform routine tasks, irresponsible actions, divorce, broken relationships, rejection by loved ones and friends, sickness, injury or other health problems) that are proof that you were in bondage, that your situation was hopeless and that you were helpless to do anything about it.

How has your addiction affected your...
Social life?

Personal life?

Spiritual life?

Physical health?

Finances?

Marriage (if married)?

Personal relationships?

Sex life?

Job or career?

The way you feel about yourself?

The way others feel about you?

When did you first believe that you were an addict?

Do you remember the time when the reality of your addiction became clear in your mind and you accepted it as a fact? Can you describe the situation? Where were you and what was going on at the time? Describe it in as much detail as you can.

What were you thinking at the time?

How did you feel about yourself?

How did you feel about your problem?

How did you feel about your future?

What did you believe about yourself at the time (i.e. what was your self-perception)?

What do you presently believe about yourself and your addiction?

Note: Everybody who struggles with addictive behaviors holds many beliefs about themselves that are not consistent with who they really are in Christ. The devil accuses you day and night, the world says you are an addict and the flesh screams in your mind that you are a no-good sinner and worthless in the sight of God. These are the lies that will keep you in bondage. The ultimate lie is to believe that freedom from your sinful addictive behavior is not possible.

C. Discovering the Truth That Sets You Free

First Things First

Before you go any further, you need to make sure that you are in a right relationship with God. Because if you're not, none of the following will mean anything to you. Have you received Jesus Christ as your Lord and Savior? The ultimate test is found in 2 Corinthians 13:5, "Test yourselves to see if you are in the faith; examine yourselves! Or do you not recognize this about yourselves, that Jesus Christ is in you—unless indeed you fail the test?"

Is Christ in you? Have you trusted in His death on the cross as payment for your sins? If you have, then you pass the test because John 1:12 says, "But as many as received Him, to them He gave the right to become children of God, even to those who believe in His name."

If you are not sure, you can receive Christ right now. Turn to Him, confess that you are a sinner, and ask Him to forgive you of your sins and come into your life. When you do this, you can be sure Christ has come into your life, your sins are forgiven and you have been given eternal life. Notice the assurance that Paul gives from Romans 10:9-13:

That if you confess with your mouth Jesus as Lord, and believe in your heart that God raised Him from the dead, you shall be saved; for with the heart man believes, resulting in righteousness, and with the mouth he confesses, resulting in salvation. For the Scripture says, "WHOEVER BELIEVES IN HIM WILL NOT BE DISAPPOINTED." For there is no distinction between Jew and Greek; for the same Lord is Lord of all, abounding in riches for all who call upon Him; for "WHOEVER WILL CALL UPON THE NAME OF THE LORD WILL BE SAVED."

Do you believe that salvation only means that our sins are forgiven and we get a ticket to heaven and therefore miss hell? While this is certainly true, there is so much more to salvation than that. We need to understand all that we have received in salvation through Christ by faith or we will fall far short of our potential. If we knew that we were totally forgiven, were justified before God and therefore at peace with Him (see Romans 5:1), and could now approach God with clean hearts (see Hebrews 10:22), we would live differently. He didn't just save us from our sins, He gave us eternal life which means that our soul and spirit are in union with Him. It is "Christ in you, the hope of glory" (Colossians 1:27). Eternal life is not something we get when we die. "He who has the Son has the life; he who does not have the Son of God does not have the life" (1 John 5:12).

In the Bible the most common words for salvation—*yeshva* (Hebrew) and *soteria* (Greek)—come from root words meaning "to deliver or to save." *Strong's Exhaustive Concordance of the Bible*[2] defines it as "rescue, or safety." *Vine's Expository Dictionary of the New Testament*[3] says that *soteria* denotes "deliverance, preservation and salvation." It also carries the definite idea of victory. Are you experiencing all the deliverance, rescue, safety, preservation and victory that God intends for you? The book of Hebrews warns us not to take our salvation lightly. Hebrews 2:3 warns us: "How shall we escape if we neglect so great a salvation?" What is God's plan and purpose for you in this great salvation?

Note: The key to freedom is knowing the truth. Pray the following prayer adapted from Ephesians 1:17-19 before you begin the section of discovering the truth that sets you free:

My glorious heavenly Father and my Lord Jesus Christ, Give me the Spirit of wisdom and revelation, so that I may know You better. I pray also that the eyes of my heart may be enlightened in order that I may know the hope to which You have called me, the riches of Your glorious inheritance in all the saints and Your incomparably great power which You extend to all of us who believe.

After each of the following verses, write what God says He plans for you in this great salvation:

"[God] has saved us, and called us with a holy calling, not according to our works, but according to His own purpose and grace which was granted us in Christ Jesus from all eternity" (2 Timothy 1:9).

"For God has not destined us for wrath, but for obtaining salvation through our Lord Jesus Christ" (1 Thessalonians 5:9).

"Obtaining as the outcome of your faith the salvation of your souls" (1 Peter 1:9).

"But we should always give thanks to God for you, brethren beloved by the Lord, because God has chosen you, [put your name here], from the beginning for salvation through sanctification by the Spirit and faith in the truth" (2 Thessalonians 2:13).

God's Word tells us that one of the primary reasons Christ came was to deliver us from bondage. In the following verses, what does it say God has delivered us from and what did He deliver us to?

      Delivered us from...   Delivered us to...

John 5:24

1 Peter 2:9

According to Luke 4:14-21, what are the five things that Christ came to do in you?

After each of the following verses, write what you are delivered and saved from:

"'For God so loved the world, that He gave His only begotten Son, that whoever believes in Him should not perish, but have eternal life. For God did not send the Son into the world to judge the world, but that the world should be saved through Him'" (John 3:16,17).

"'And she will bear a Son; and you shall call His name Jesus, for it is He who will save His people from their sins'" (Matthew 1:21).

"Much more then, having now been justified by His blood, we shall be saved from the wrath of God through Him" (Romans 5:9).

"Salvation from our enemies, and from the hand of all who hate us" (Luke 1:71).

"Who gave Himself for our sins, that He might deliver us out of this present evil age, according to the will of our God and Father" (Galatians 1:4).

"Since then the children share in flesh and blood, He Himself likewise also partook of the same, that through death He might render powerless him who had the power of death, that is, the devil; and might deliver those who through fear of death were subject to slavery all their lives" (Hebrews 2:14,15).

Note: We are not in this present mental, emotional, spiritual and physical state because of what has happened to us. We are in this present condition because of how we chose to interpret life situations and consequently respond to them. Do you believe that freedom from addiction is really possible? In writing to the Galatians, Paul makes it clear that Christ has given us freedom, but it is possible for us to be entangled again in bondage rather than experience freedom. "It was for freedom that Christ set us free; therefore keep standing firm and do not be subject again to a yoke of slavery" (Galatians 5:1).

When you first became a Christian, did you experience this freedom? What was different in your life? Be specific.

When you first became a Christian, did you believe that God would free you from your addiction?

How have your beliefs changed since then?

As you have struggled and failed to overcome addictive behaviors, what have you believed about yourself and your ability to overcome sin?

Are these beliefs in line with the truth of God's Word?

Perhaps you are thinking, *If I am delivered and set free, why don't I feel like it and act like it?* Good question. That will be addressed in section D. But first one more look at freedom:

> "Jesus therefore was saying to those Jews who had believed Him, 'If you abide in My word, then you are truly disciples of Mine; and you shall know the truth, and the truth shall make you free.' They answered Him, 'We are Abraham's off-

spring, and have never yet been enslaved to anyone; how is it that You say, "You shall become free"?' Jesus answered them, 'Truly, truly, I say to you, everyone who commits sin is the slave of sin. And the slave does not remain in the house forever; the son does remain forever. If therefore the Son shall make you free, you shall be free indeed'" (John 8:31-36).

According to Jesus, what still enslaves us?

How can we be freed from this enslavement?

If knowing truth makes you free, then believing lies will keep you in bondage. What are the lies that have kept you in bondage?

In John 8:36, Jesus makes a very definitive and conclusive statement about freedom. Perhaps like me you have looked in a lot of places and tried a lot of things, but Christ is the only one who can set you completely free.

It was for freedom that Christ set you free and when He sets you free, you are *really* free. However, it is possible to fall back into the same old habits, but you don't have to stay there. Freedom is part of the salvation package. It's your birthright as a child of God. Don't let the enemy rob you of what is rightfully yours. Freedom is part of your inheritance. Don't settle for less!

D. Stating the Truth

How would you state the truth that you have learned in the previous section? Take some time to review and write it out. Stay true to God's Word, but don't be afraid to make it personal, practical and applicable to your situation. Examples of some of the truth would be:

Christ came to set me free from my sins and gave me a new life in Him.

I am no longer a product of my past; I am a new creation in Christ.

I am not an addict or codependent. I may struggle with some of those behaviors, but I am now a child of God.

State additional truths you have learned:

Think of a situation in the past that turned out badly. How could the situation have been changed if you had believed these truths and applied them?

> **The Truth:**
> Freedom from all sin, including the bondage of
> addiction, is the birthright of every child of God.

E. Illustrating the Truth ················

To illustrate these truths refer to pages 126-127 in *Freedom from Addiction* beginning with "Zig Ziglar relates..." and ending with "...make no effort to enter."

What kept Houdini locked in the jail cell for so long?

What did he need to believe to walk out free?

Do you see that the only thing that kept Houdini locked in the jail cell was believing the lie that the door was locked? It would not have helped if he had tried harder, been more positive, changed his attitude, been more committed or even been a better person.

Have you perhaps been working hard to get something that has already been given you? Maybe you were not aware that the prison door is no longer locked. But the good news—that is what the word "gospel" means—is that Christ has unlocked the door. But if the enemy can deceive you into believing it is locked, you will never get out. Someone has said that the two biggest mistakes Christians make are: First, trying to get something they already have, and second, trying to be someone they already are.

I (Mike) tried everything I knew to try, but all to no avail. If you have completed the reading of *Freedom from Addiction*, you know that on the day that I walked out of my prison of addiction, it was simply because I finally believed the truth. None of the things I tried to do on my own had helped me. As a matter of fact, I had been drunk the day before. But when I believed the truth, I was free! Jesus said, "You will know the truth, and the truth will set you free" (John 8:32, *NIV*).

F. Appropriating the Truth

To make the truth real and relevant to you, in the following chart write the lies that you have exposed, that you have been believing, and that have robbed you of your freedom. Then beside each exposed lie, write the truth you have learned. One example is given:

The Lie That Binds You	The Truth That Sets You Free
I renounce the lie that: *I will never be free.*	I announce the truth that: *Christ has set me free.*

G. Personalizing the Truth

Internalize the truth by personalizing Scripture and confessing it. Change the pronouns to personal pronouns and paraphrase the Scriptures to make them real and personal to you. For instance, "For God so loved *me,* that He gave His only begotten Son, that *I* may have eternal life" (adapted from John 3:16).

The group you are studying with will add many other verses. Develop the habit of renouncing the lies you have believed and announcing the truth out loud and often. (If you can't do it out loud, do it in your mind.) This is a powerful way to renew your mind to the truth of God's Word. An example could be: "Christ has done everything necessary for me to walk in freedom and I renounce the lie that I have to stay in bondage to this addiction. I choose to believe the truth that I am alive and free in Christ."

Look at the following example of personalizing Scripture, a prayer adapted from Ephesians 3:14-19:

> For this very reason, I bow my knees before You, heavenly Father. Every family in heaven and on earth derives its name from You. I pray that You would grant me strength and power through Your Spirit in my inner self according to the riches of Your glory, so that Christ may dwell in my heart through faith. I ask this so that I may be rooted and grounded in love and that I may be able to comprehend with all the saints what is the breadth and length and height and depth of Your love which is beyond my ability to know. I ask to be filled up with Your fullness.

Your Personal Statement of the Truth That Sets You Free

Who you are and how you live your life in the power of the Holy Spirit cannot be determined by how you feel, by what others think of you or by the circumstances of life.

Go back through this chapter and find all the negative things you thought about yourself and your situation. Then consider the truths that you have learned through this chapter. Write your personal statement of the truth that sets you free.

Notes.
1. William L. Playfair and George Bryson, *The Useful Lie*, (Wheaton, Ill.: Crossway Books, 1991), p. 185.
2. James Strong, LL.D., S.T.D., *Strong's Exhaustive Concordance of the Bible* (Nashville, Tenn.: Thomas Nelson Publishers, 1984).
3. William E. Vine, *Vine's Expository Dictionary of the New Testament* (Uhrichsville, Ohio: Barbour Books, 1989).

What Keeps You in Bondage?

The Overcomer's Covenant in Christ

Statement Two

I consciously and deliberately choose to submit to God and resist the devil by denying myself, picking up my cross daily and following Jesus. I know that my soul was never designed by God to function as the master. I know that "rebellion is as the sin of witchcraft, and stubbornness is as iniquity and idolatry" (1 Samuel 15:23, KJV).

The ultimate lie of Satan is to believe that we are God. We are not the master of our fate nor the captain of our soul. If we are not serving the true God, then we are serving the god of this world who deceives us into thinking that we are serving ourselves. It seems to be the great ambition of mankind to settle for living as animals rather than being blessed as children of God. Indulging our fleshly appetites does not satisfy them; indulgence only creates a greater dependency upon those things we crave. Only those who hunger and thirst for righteousness will be satisfied (see Matthew 5:6).

Jesus said, "For whoever wishes to save his life shall lose it; but whoever loses his life for My sake shall find it" (Matthew 16:25). Those who look for their purpose and meaning in life in the natural order of things will lose their lives. Those who find their identity, significance and security in Christ will experience real life now and for all eternity. Paul wrote, "Discipline yourself for the purpose of godliness; for bodily discipline is only of little profit, but godliness is profitable for all things since it holds promise for the present life and also for the life to come" (1 Timothy 4:7,8).

Paul instructed, "Let every person be in subjection to the governing authorities. For there is no authority except from God, and those which exist are established by God. Therefore he who resists authority has opposed the ordinance of God; and they who have opposed will receive condemnation upon themselves" (Romans 13:1,2). To win the spiritual battle we must be under God's authority. Only then can you resist the devil. Trying to resist the devil without first submitting to God will be a dog fight. Submitting to God without resisting the devil will keep you in bondage. We must first submit to God, then resist the devil and he will flee from us (see James 4:7).

A. Understanding the Problem ·········· A

In this chapter how strongholds are established in our minds and how they keep us in bondage will be explored. Have you ever had some well-meaning friend say to you about your addiction, "That's wrong. It's sin. Stop doing it"? Or maybe they have said, "Can't you see that what you are doing is destroying everything in your life that is good?" I (Mike) have heard all these pronouncements. Of course I knew what I was doing was wrong, and I wanted desperately to stop. Nobody likes to live in bondage, but I seemed powerless to break out of that crippling bondage. Why is this so? What keeps us in bondage?

All Christians know their sins have been forgiven and they're going to heaven. But in the meantime for many it is a "mean" time. Pastors I have talked with have observed that 85 percent of their people do not appear to be experiencing freedom. Most seem to believe they are locked into their old patterns of behavior because of their genetic makeup, family background and environment. In short, they believe they are victims of their pasts and circumstances. But God's Word tells us we are not products of our pasts, but we are the products of what Christ accomplished for us on the cross.

If we believe that we are victims of our past, it really won't make any difference what we do to try to get free. We always act consistently with how we perceive ourselves. Our behavior is a result of what we believe about ourselves, God and the world we live in. I (Mike) teach at a Christian treatment center and the one thing that I always tell those I teach is, "It won't help or matter if you work the program perfectly. *If* you do not change the way you think and believe, you will fail." Many have worked the programs the best they could and left with high hopes, yet ended up falling back into their addictive behaviors in a matter of days, weeks or months. Why? All they changed was their behavior for a few months. The old belief system that had them locked into bondage was still intact.

What about you? Who are you? Are you a product of your family environment, your genetic makeup and all that has gone on in your life up to this point? Is your past the determining factor in who you are and what you do? Most people would answer in the affirmative. But when you became a Christian, you became a new creation in Christ (see 2 Corinthians 5:17) and a partaker of the divine nature (see 2 Peter 1:4). You are not the same person you were before. "Therefore if any man is in Christ, he is a new creature; the old things passed away; behold, new things have come" (2 Corinthians 5:17). You are no longer living in the flesh; you are living in Christ (see Romans 8:9). But before we look at the truth of who you really are, let's take a look at the lies you have believed that have kept you in bondage.

B. Making a Personal Appraisal

We are all born with certain basic needs. Our biggest needs are to be loved and accepted, and to have a sense of worth. Others have defined the basic needs differently using terms such as security, belonging and significance, but all would fit into the acrostic **LAW: L**ove, **A**cceptance and **W**orth. These are universal needs which have to be met in order to live a victorious and fruitful life.

God's plan is for us to have a living relationship with Him and for us to look to Him to meet our needs according to His riches in glory. But when we were born into this world, we didn't have a relationship with God. So we attempted to meet our needs the best way we knew how. We learned how to cope, succeed, survive and defend ourselves independent from God. That is essentially the character of the flesh, or old nature. We don't automatically stop living that way when we become Christians. In fact, many still continue to operate in the flesh, not realizing they are doing so. The lifelong, deeply entrenched flesh patterns can develop into mental strongholds that keep us from experiencing the freedom that Christ purchased for us on the cross. The following exercise will enable you to determine the ways that you have learned to live independent from God. Many believe this is just the way we are and that we will never change. As long as we believe that, we will never change.

This will be the longest and hardest exercise you will do, but it is essential for your freedom. You are going to be exposing the primary lies that have kept you in bondage. It will also be the most painful, and you may be tempted to rush through it. But keep in mind that the power of a lie is broken when we expose it to the light.

Your Family Background

List and briefly describe any traumatic childhood memories or impacting events that took place that you witnessed or were involved in. You may need to answer these questions on separate sheets of paper. (Note: The use of the + and * symbols will be explained later in this exercise. Do not be concerned with their use as you answer the questions.)

Describe each situation and location where it happened.

Who were the villains or heroes? What did they do or not do?

*How did you respond to the situation?

+Describe the emotional impact it had on you.

+How did it make you feel about yourself then?

+How does it make you feel about yourself now?

+How did this affect your self-perception?

*How did this affect your perception of other people?

*As a result, what kind of outlook on life do you have?

Describe your family life from birth to twelve years of age. How would you describe the atmosphere in your home?

+How would you describe yourself as a child?

Your Relationship with Your Father:

Describe your relationship with your father during your childhood.

Did he spend quality time alone with you? Why or why not and how did that make you feel toward him?

+How did that make you feel about yourself?

How would you describe your father's personality, temperament and character?

How did your father communicate to you by...
Showing affection?

Praise or affirmation?

Criticism (what did he criticize you or others for)?

+How did it make you feel about yourself when he criticized you?

*How did you handle it when he criticized you (i.e. did you clam up, argue, make excuses, promise yourself to try harder, defend yourself, give up, etc.)?

Summarize the most hurtful things he ever did or said to you.

+How do you think this affected your self-perception?

Describe how your relationship with your father (good or bad) has had a positive or detrimental effect on how you perceive yourself, others and life in general.

Your Relationship with Your Mother:

Describe your relationship with your mother during your childhood.

Did she spend quality time alone with you? Why or why not, and how did that make you feel toward her?

How would you describe your mother's personality, temperament and character?

How did your mother communicate to you by...
Showing affection?

Praise or affirmation?

Criticism (what did she criticize you or others for)?

+How did it make you feel about yourself when she criticized you?

*How did you handle it when she criticized you (i.e., did you clam up, argue, make excuses, promise yourself to try harder, defend yourself, give up, etc.)?

Summarize the most hurtful things she ever did to you or said to you.

+How do you think this affected your self-perception?

Can you see how your relationship with your mother (good or bad) has had a positive or detrimental effect on how you perceive yourself, others, and life in general?

Your Relationships with Your Siblings:

List your siblings in birth order (oldest to youngest) and where you fit into that order.

What were the most hurtful things they did to you?

+How did this make you feel about yourself?

*+Did your father have a favorite child? If so, who was it and how do you feel about it?

+How did it affect the way you related to your family?

*+Did your mother have a favorite child? If so, who was it and how do you feel about it?

+How did it affect the way you related to your family?

For what did you and each of your siblings get criticized, affirmed or singled out by your parents?

Your Parents' Relationships with Each Other:

How did your father treat your mother?

How did she respond to him?

Did your father treat women with respect?

Did your mother treat men with respect?

Was your father the leader in the home or were the roles reversed?

From the way they related to each other, what did you learn:

+About yourself?

About men?

About women?

About relationships?

About marriage?

*+How did you respond at the time when family conflicts arose?

*+How has that affected you?

*How do you handle conflict?

Who was the disciplinarian in your home when you were growing up?
How did that person discipline you?

*Did your mom and dad teach you responsibility and that you must face the consequences of your actions? How has that affected your life?

Did they provide guidance and direction concerning the important issues in life (i.e., moral choices, school, relationships, sex, dating, church, work, career, health, etc.)? In what areas would you have liked for them to have given you more guidance and direction?

*How has their instruction and guidance (or lack thereof) affected your life?

*+What is your best childhood memory and how have good childhood memories affected your self-perception and attitudes about life?

Your Responses to Life Situations:

How do you respond in public to the following situations (i.e. try to ignore it, clam up, express yourself, blame someone, etc.)?

*When you are publicly embarrassed?

*When someone has hurt you emotionally or physically?

*When a person or circumstance makes you angry?

*When you think you have failed?

*When someone threatens you?

*When someone disappoints you?

Broken Relationships

Make a list of all estranged relationships that were at one time meaningful to you, including spouses or former marriage partners, parents
and employers. Write by each name how you felt after the breakup of
the relationship. You may need to use a separate piece of paper for this
exercise.

Estranged Relationship	+How the failed relationship affected my self-perception	*How the experience affected my attitude toward life

Summarize how broken relationships and experiences of rejection have affected your self-perception and sense of worth.

Employment Experiences

List each job you have had, beginning with part-time and summer jobs. Was each one a good or a bad experience? How did you and each of your supervisors get along? Beside each one, write out what you learned about yourself and about life from your experience. You may need to use a separate piece of paper for this exercise.

Employment Experience	+How that work experience affected my self-perception	*How that job affected my attitude toward life

Summary

To see how living in this fallen world without Christ has developed flesh patterns in your mind, complete the "Summary of My False Identity and Flesh Patterns" chart on page 59 by following these steps:

STEP ONE: Go back through all your answers and look at those with a + beside the question. Each one of these answers will show how you felt about yourself and the messages you were believing. Record all the feelings that you had about yourself. These are the bases for forming impressions about yourself which in most cases are not true according to who you are in Christ. We don't want you to deny your past or present feelings. That is never healthy. We just want to help you see how negative experiences can wrongly shape our self-perception.

STEP TWO: Read the following list of words. Put a check mark by any of those feelings or attitudes that you have had toward yourself. Then put all those checked on the chart on page 59 as well. If you are not sure, do not put something down just because you may have felt like it only occasionally in the past. Probably all of us have had each one of these attitudes or feelings about ourselves at some time. Look for those words that describe you or what you have felt about yourself that have negatively affected your self-image. As you continue through this workbook, other negative feelings or attitudes may emerge that you can add to the list later.

Negative Feelings

❏ inadequate	❏ insecure	❏ inferior
❏ unwanted	❏ unloved	❏ bad, evil
❏ unaccepted	❏ unimportant	❏ guilty
❏ worthless	❏ rejected	❏ abandoned
❏ helpless	❏ hopeless	❏ stupid, dumb
❏ insignificant	❏ nobody	❏ no good

This list is not exhaustive, but is an example of the lies that we believe about ourselves. Since we were all born spiritually dead—separated from God (see Ephesians 2:1)—our natural identity was derived from the fallen world. Satan, the god of this world, accuses the brethren day and night (see Revelation 12:9-11). He can't do anything about our position in Christ, but if he can get us to believe that we are nothing more than a product of our past, we will live as though that is true, and we will be defeated. With most of us, he has done a real good job and we have bought the lie that the old nature is who we are. The truth is we are alive to God in Christ and dead to sin (see Romans 6:11) and we are to consider it so for the rest of our lives by taking every thought captive to the obedience of Christ (see 2 Corinthians 10:5).

STEP THREE: Go back through all your answers and look for those that have a * before them. These answers indicate your flesh patterns—how you learned to cope, succeed or survive and meet your needs independent from God. Write these flesh patterns you have developed on the "Summary of My False Identity and Flesh Patterns" chart.

STEP FOUR: Look over the following list of what we call "flesh patterns." These are coping mechanisms that we use to keep us living independent from God. Read through the list and put a check mark by any of the mechanisms that have been a means to meet your needs for acceptance, security and significance, or a means to cope, succeed and survive. Don't check a word or phrase if it hasn't been a pattern in your life. You can always come back and check it off later. It might be helpful to reread Chapter 2 in *Freedom from Addiction* and see how my (Mike's) flesh patterns developed.

Flesh Patterns

- ❑ Alcoholism
- ❑ Argumentative
- ❑ Arrogant
- ❑ Avoid intimacy
- ❑ Avoid others
- ❑ Blame others
- ❑ Boastful
- ❑ Bossy
- ❑ Complacent
- ❑ Compulsive behavior
- ❑ Compulsive thoughts
- ❑ Conceit
- ❑ Controlled by emotions
- ❑ Covetousness
- ❑ Critical
- ❑ Deceitful
- ❑ Defensive
- ❑ Deny feelings
- ❑ Deny reality
- ❑ Depression
- ❑ Dominance
- ❑ Drug dependency
- ❑ Envy
- ❑ False modesty
- ❑ Exaggeration
- ❑ Fear
- ❑ Fear of failure
- ❑ Gluttony
- ❑ Greed
- ❑ Gossip
- ❑ Gushy
- ❑ Hateful
- ❑ Hold grudges
- ❑ Hostile
- ❑ Idolatry
- ❑ Impulsive
- ❑ Impure thoughts
- ❑ Indecisive

- ❑ Indifferent
- ❑ Intimidate people
- ❑ Introspective
- ❑ Irresponsible
- ❑ Irritable
- ❑ Jealous
- ❑ Lazy
- ❑ Loner
- ❑ Lying
- ❑ Manipulative
- ❑ Materialistic
- ❑ Moody
- ❑ Negativism
- ❑ Obsessive-Compulsive
- ❑ Opinionated
- ❑ Overly submissive
- ❑ Overly sensitive to criticism
- ❑ Passive
- ❑ Passive-aggressive
- ❑ People-pleaser
- ❑ Possessive of things/others
- ❑ Perfectionist
- ❑ Pretentious
- ❑ Prejudice
- ❑ Pride
- ❑ Procrastination
- ❑ Profane
- ❑ Rebellious
- ❑ Resentful
- ❑ Restless
- ❑ Revengeful
- ❑ Sadness
- ❑ Sarcastic
- ❑ Seductive behavior
- ❑ Self-condemning
- ❑ Self-depreciation
- ❑ Self-hatred
- ❑ Self-indulgence

- ❑ Self-justification
- ❑ Self-pity
- ❑ Self-righteous
- ❑ Self-serving
- ❑ Self-sufficient
- ❑ Self-reliant
- ❑ Selfish ambition
- ❑ Sensuality
- ❑ Sexual fantasy
- ❑ Sexual lust
- ❑ Silent treatment
- ❑ Slanderous
- ❑ Stubborn
- ❑ Subjective
- ❑ Suicidal thoughts
- ❑ Surly
- ❑ Suspicious
- ❑ Temper
- ❑ Unable to receive love
- ❑ Vanity
- ❑ Withdrawal
- ❑ Workaholic
- ❑ Worrier

Summary of My False Identity and Flesh Patterns

My False Identity—

As a result of the messages I received and believed about myself from the experiences I have had, these are the lies I have believed that have formed a false basis for my identity and sense of worth. I have believed that I am...

My Flesh Patterns—

As a result of believing these lies, I have learned to meet my needs for acceptance, security, worth and value. I have tried to cope, succeed, achieve, defend myself, protect myself, escape, avoid failure, deal with stress and live my life independent from God by...

STEP FIVE: Look at your completed chart. Do you see how you have been programmed by the world, the flesh and the devil to be in bondage? Do you realize that as long as you keep believing these lies and living according to the flesh, you will stay in bondage?

But that is not who you are or how you have to live. You developed these flesh patterns by trying to meet your own needs and survive in life independent from God. Satan will seek to control you through your flesh patterns, but you do not have to believe Satan's lies and respond in the flesh.

Ask God to show you how you have been kept in bondage by the enemy and to open your eyes to the truth that sets you free. What keeps you in bondage is believing the lie that you are nothing more than a product of your past.

C. Discovering the Truth That Sets You Free

What is truth? What does God's Word have to say? Remember that the key to freedom is knowing the truth. Before beginning this section, pray the following prayer adapted from Ephesians 1:17-19:

> Dear Heavenly Father,
> I keep asking that You would give me the Spirit of wisdom and revelation, so that I may know You better. I pray also that the eyes of my heart may be enlightened in order that I may know the hope to which You have called me, and the riches of Your glorious inheritance in the saints, and Your incomparably great power for us who believe. In Jesus' name, I pray. Amen.

If it is true that our perception of ourselves determines how we live, then it is critically important to know who we are. Are we just a product of our genetic makeup, our family background and all the experiences of our lives? Are we bound to our past? Will it determine who we are and how we live for the rest of our lives? Did Jesus' death on the cross accomplish any more than forgiveness of sins and a ticket to heaven?

Redemption is more than an important biblical word or concept. Thousands of years ago, Job said, "'And as for me, I know that my Redeemer lives, and at the last He will take His stand on the earth'" (Job 19:25). David wrote, "Let the words of my mouth and the meditation of my heart be acceptable in Thy sight, O LORD, my rock and my Redeemer" (Psalms 19:14). And God told us, "'And I will feed your oppressors with their own flesh, and they will become drunk with their own blood as with sweet wine; and all flesh will know that I, the LORD, am your Savior, and your Redeemer, the Mighty One of Jacob'" (Isaiah 49:26).

The Greek word *lutroo* literally means "to set free, redeem, rescue" (from Bauer, et al, *A Greek-English Lexicon of the New Testament and Other Early Christian Literature*[1]). *Strong's*[2] definition is "to loosen with a redemption price as in a ransom." *Vine's*[3] says it means "to buy out, especially with a view to freedom."

Read Luke 1:68 and Romans 5:8,9. Who accomplished the redemption and who or what was redeemed?

Look up the verses below and write beside each reference what you have been redeemed from:

Psalm 103:4 _____

Galatians 3:18 _____

Galatians 4:5 _____

Colossians 1:13 _____

Colossians 1:21,22 _____

Titus 2:14 _____

Hebrews 2:15 _____

Hebrews 9:12-14 _____

One of the definitions of redemption is "freedom obtained by the payment of a ransom." Read Acts 20:28, Galatians 2:20 and Ephesians 1:7. What was the price paid for your redemption?

According to Romans 5:6, who was this great redemption for?

Read the following verses and write beside each reference what God has done about your past:

Romans 6:4

2 Corinthians 5:17

Galatians 1:4

1 Peter 1:18,19

What is God's purpose for you now?

Read Galatians 4:3-9. What has God redeemed you from in order to be someone very special?

What are the characteristics of this special person?

Galatians 4:9 asks the question, "But now that you have come to know God, or rather to be known by God, how is it that you turn back to the weak and worthless elemental things, to which you desire to be enslaved all over again?" Why do you think people go back into bondage?

Why do you think *you* went back into bondage after salvation in Christ?

Read 1 John 3:1-3 which tells us who we are and where our hope lies, and then read 2 Peter 1:3-10 which reveals the cause of failing to grow in Christ. What do you think you had forgotten regarding your purification from your former sins, or what had you never known about your redemption and who you are in Christ that made it possible for you to go back into bondage?

D. Stating the Truth

> **The Truth:**
> I am not a product of my past, but I am a product of the
> work of Christ on the cross and I can now rest in His
> finished work, walk by the Spirit and not carry out
> the desires of the flesh.

E. Illustrating the Truth

To illustrate these truths, refer to the story of the Emancipation Proclamation and the slaves in *Freedom from Addiction* pages 239-241 beginning with "Slavery in the United States..." and ending with "...the One who set him free."

Paul says, "Knowing this, that our old self was crucified with Him, that our body of sin might be done away with, that we should no longer be slaves to sin; for he who has died [with Christ] is freed from sin" (Romans 6:6,7). Have you died with Christ? Then you are free from sin. Do you believe it? How does this passage and story of the freed slaves relate to your addiction?

F. Appropriating the Truth

In order to make the truth real and relevant to you, write down the lies that you have been believing that rob you of your freedom. Then write down the truth you have learned that sets you free. One example is given:

The Lie That Binds You	The Truth That Sets You Free
I renounce the lie that: *I am a product of my past.*	I announce the truth that: *I am a product of the Cross.*

G. Personalizing the Truth ·············

Internalize the truth by personalizing Scripture and confessing it.

For example:
By dying on the cross for me and making me a new creation, Christ has redeemed me from the empty way of life that I learned from growing up in my family and all the other experiences that led me to believe I was a hopeless addict (see 1 Peter 1:18,19 and 2 Corinthians 5:17).

Personalize the following Scriptures and any others that God has given you about your new life in Him.

Ephesians 1:3-13

Colossians 2:6-10

1 John 3:1-3

Stay in the habit of renouncing the lies you have believed and announcing the truth out loud and often. (If you can't do it out loud, do it in your mind.)

Notes:

1. Walter Bauer, et al, Translated from the German by William F. Arndt, *A Greek-English Lexicon of the New Testament and Other Early Christian Literature* (Chicago, Ill.: University of Chicago Press, 1979).
2. James Strong, LL.D., S.T.D., *Strong's Exhaustive Concordance of the Bible* (Nashville, Tenn.: Thomas Nelson Publishers, 1984).
3. William E. Vine, *Vine's Expository Dictionary of the New Testament* (Uhrichsville, Ohio: Barbour Books, 1989).

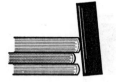

Reading Assignment: Chapters 3 and 4 in *Freedom from Addiction*

Giving Up on Self

....

The Overcomer's Covenant in Christ

Statement Three

I choose to humble myself before the mighty hand of God in order that He may exalt me at the proper time. I know that God is opposed to the proud but gives grace to the humble (see James 4:6).

Pride says, "I can get out of this by myself. I don't need God or anyone else. When it comes to drinking (or using, overeating, etc.), I can stop any time I want." The only way to prove that, of course, is to stop. Pride refuses to acknowledge our need for God and each other. The truth is, we absolutely need God and we necessarily need each other. Our pride will rob us of the grace of God. We must humble ourselves by walking in the light (see 1 John 1:6,7), and speaking the truth in love for we are members of one Body (see Ephesians 4:25). Not to do so would give the devil a foothold in our lives (see Ephesians 4:27, *NIV*).

Someone cannot be helped unless he or she is willing to admit that there is a need for help. Even the Lord intends to pass by the self-sufficient (see Mark 6:48). If you want to row your own boat against the storms of life, He will let you. Only those who call upon the name of the Lord will be saved (see 1 Corinthians 1:2). Brokenness is the essential prerequisite to victory. As long as people in bondage can hide their sin, they likely will. Eventually those who lie and cover up their addictions will be exposed: "For nothing is hidden, except to be revealed; nor has anything been secret, but that it should come to light"

(Mark 4:22). Secret sin on earth is open scandal in heaven. It is better to "Humble yourselves in the presence of the Lord, and He will exalt you" (James 4:10).

A. Understanding the Problem ···········

No one plans to be an addict, nor prefers to live hopelessly in bondage. I (Mike) certainly didn't plan on it. I desperately wanted to be free. I tried anything and everything anyone told me to do. The following is a list of things that I tried. My wife, Julia, told me I had earned a Doctorate in Drunkenness.

What I Did to Try to Free Myself from Addiction

1. Consistent quiet time
2. Bible study
3. Fasting
4. Visitation evangelism
5. Christian 12-Step Program
6. Accountability group
7. Hundreds of AA meetings and five different sponsors
8. Christian counselors
9. Christian psychiatrist
10. Secular psychiatrist
11. Christian psychologist
12. Secular psychologist
13. Addiction counselor
14. Flew to New Jersey to spend three days with a specialist
15. Secular treatment center
16. Christian treatment center
17. Read every book on addiction
18. Healing of Memories session
19. Baptism of the Spirit session
20. Casting out of demons session, twice
21. Public confession
22. Group therapy
23. Took the drug Antabuse
24. Disciplined by my church
25. Rigid schedule with every minute planned
26. Hundreds of hours studying scriptural principles
27. Memorized chapters of Scripture
28. Discipleship groups
29. Prayer
30. Promises to God and my wife

Why didn't any of these work for me? Because I tried everything but the person of Christ and His resources. God's purpose is not to help us get stronger by ourselves so we can handle everything by ourselves. His purpose is to show us how weak and incomplete we are in the flesh so that we will give up on ourselves and turn to Him to be our strength and wisdom. He brought me to the end of my resources in order that I might discover His. Self-control is a fruit of the Spirit, not the result of self-help programs and superhuman effort. Our own pride is what keeps us from experiencing freedom in Christ.

 ········· # B. Making a Personal Appraisal

How have you personally tried to cope with or get free of your addiction? List everything that you have tried or are presently trying.

Why do you think these things you have tried haven't worked for you? Was it...

☐ Lack of willpower   ☐ Lack of knowledge
☐ Lack of finances   ☐ Lack of other resources
☐ Lack of character (moral) ☐ Lack of opportunity
☐ Lack of support   ☐ Lack of education
☐ Lack of _____

What do you believe you need to do to be free?

What do you think must happen for you to be free from your addiction?

If you listed anything that you need to do, it will probably be another thing you will have to add to your list of what you tried that didn't work. What do you believe is God's purpose for you as a Christian?

What are *you* depending on and trying to do now to overcome your addiction?

What other resources, programs, treatments, methods, groups, etc. could you try that you haven't yet tried?

What have loved ones, relatives and friends done or said that have kept you from coming to the end of yourself and your resources? In other words how have they enabled you to continue in your addiction or encouraged you in the wrong direction?

What do you think would have to happen for you to come to the point where you finally realize that there is nothing you can do to save yourself or set yourself free?

How much do you think you would have to lose in order to come to that point?

Are you willing to totally trust God to do for you what you cannot do for yourself, no matter how hard you try? If not, why not?

Note: Realize that God loves you and is at this very moment willing to supply you with all the power and self-control you need to live a free and victorious life. But if you prefer to do it yourself, He will let you. He will not force His will upon you. You have to choose to say "Thy will be done." To not do so is nothing more than sinful pride or deceptive ignorance.

Some strong-willed people have to hit the bottom. They will not surrender their will until they have lost everything meaningful to them (their family, career, health, etc.). Willpower is a deadly deception. Willpower *is* the answer, but you need *His will* and *His power*. As long as you are relying on your strength and resources, neither this workbook nor any other program will help you get free. No book, program or group can be a substitute for God Himself. The right books, programs and groups are those that teach you to be dependent upon your loving heavenly Father.

> **The Lie:**
> **I can do it myself. All I have to do is try harder,**
> **get stronger and learn how to cope or deal**
> **with my addiction.**

C. Discovering the Truth That Sets You Free

Remember that the key to freedom is knowing the truth. Pray the following prayer adapted from Ephesians 1:17-19 before you begin this section of discovering the truth that sets you free.

Dear Heavenly Father,

I am asking again that You would give me the Spirit of wisdom and revelation, so that I may know You better. I pray also that the eyes of my heart may be enlightened in order that I may know the hope to which You have called me, the riches of Your glorious inheritance in the saints and Your incomparably great power for us who believe. In Jesus name, I pray. Amen.

The Great Omission

Read Matthew 16:21-27. Peter, the noble confessor of the fundamental truth that Jesus is the Christ (the Messiah), the Son of the Living God (Deity), suddenly finds himself in league with the powers of darkness, the unconscious mouthpiece of Satan the deceiver. This memorable rebuke seems mercilessly severe, yet even the crediting of Satan as the source describes exactly and appropriately the character of the advice given by Peter which was essentially this: "Save yourself at any rate; sacrifice duty to self-interest, the cause of Christ to personal convenience." This advice is truly Satanic in principle for the whole aim of Satan is to get self-interest recognized as the chief end of man. Satan is called the prince of this world because he is the prince of self-interest and self-interest rules the world. He is called the accuser of the brethren because he does not want the children of God to believe that they can have any higher motive than serving themselves.

Did Job or even Jesus serve God for nothing? Self-sacrifice, suffering for righteousness sake and commitment to truth even unto death is pure romance and youthful sentimentalism or at best hypocritical. There is no such thing as a surrender of the lower life for the higher; all men are selfish at heart and have their price. Some may hold out longer than others, but in the end everyone prefers to do his or her own thing rather than submit to God. Such is Satan's creed. Man unwittingly serves Satan by being deceived into thinking that he is serving self. Jesus counters Satan's deception by sharing the way of the Cross and the repudiation of self.

How would you explain the way of the Cross (see Matthew 16:24)?

What does it mean to deny self?

Note: Denying self is not the same as self-denial. You can deny yourself certain things like food or clothing, but that is not the same as denying self. To deny self you need to understand your natural life's enmity with God (see Jeremiah 17:9; Romans 7:18; Ephesians 2:1-3). You have learned to live your life independent from God, and every temptation is an attempt by the devil to get you to continue living as though you are your own god. Your soul was never designed to function as the master. You are either serving mammon or the Lord Jesus Christ (see Matthew 6:24). Self-seeking, self-serving, self-justifying, self-glorifying, self-centered and self-confident living are in actuality serving the world, the flesh and the devil (see Luke 11:23; 1 John 2:15-17; 5:19; Revelation 12:9).

What does it mean to pick up your cross daily?

Note: You are forgiven because He died in your place; you are delivered because you have died with Him. The Cross provides forgiveness for what you have done but also deliverance from what you were.

What do you think Jesus meant when He said, "Follow Me"?

Note: Self-will never casts out self; we have to be led into it by the Holy Spirit. "For we who live are constantly being delivered over to death for Jesus' sake, that the life of Jesus also may be manifested in our mortal flesh" (2 Corinthians 4:11).

The Victory of the Cross

The concept of lordship seems negative to many people, but if you make Jesus the Lord of your life, He becomes the Lord of your past, present and future. He is the Lord of your problems, your defense against the devil, your power for victorious living and your assurance for the future. In a similar fashion, surrendering everything to Him seems so austere and negative to some. But what are you really sacrificing? Read Matthew 16:25-27, then comment on the following statements and answer the questions:

> You are sacrificing the lower life to gain the higher (see v. 25).

Why is it the great ambition of man to be content to live like animals instead of being blessed as children of God?

> You are sacrificing the pleasure of things to gain the pleasure of life (see v. 26).

What would you exchange for love, joy, peace, patience, kindness, goodness, faithfulness, gentleness and self-control which are the fruit of the Spirit? A new car? A promotion? Social status? A Ph.D.?

> You are sacrificing the temporal to gain the eternal (v. 27).

Jim Elliot said, "He is no fool who gives up what he cannot keep in order to gain what he cannot lose." The Christian life is full of paradoxes to the natural mind. The path to glorification is death (see John 12:23-26); the path to exaltation is humiliation (see Philippians 2:8,9); if one wishes to save his life, he must lose it (see Matthew 16:24-27); the first shall be last; etc. The natural man balks at such notions because "they are foolishness to him, and he cannot understand them, because they are spiritually appraised" (1 Corinthians 2:14).

Satan "deceives the whole world" (Revelation 12:9) and has "blinded the minds of the unbelieving" (2 Corinthians 4:4) so that man will exchange "the truth of God for a lie" (Romans 1:25). His deceptions and lies have resulted in people being "destroyed for lack of knowledge" (see Hosea 4:6). The greatest evidence of this can be seen in the failure of Christians to live a victorious life. Statements like "the Christian life is impossible" and "I'm only human" reflect a faulty belief system. We have been delivered from the kingdom of darkness to the kingdom of light and God has provided for us all the necessary resources which are made effective by virtue of our union with Christ. The truth that we have been saved not by how we behave but by how we believe is a paradox and stumbling block to the natural mind. The reality of that truth is the basis for freedom and conquest through our union with Christ and our walk by faith.

> Earthly thrones are generally built with steps up to them; the remarkable thing about the thrones of the eternal kingdom is that the steps are all down to them. We must descend if we would reign, stoop if we would rise, gird ourselves to wash the feet of the disciples as a common slave in order to share the royalty of our Divine Master. —F.B. Meyer

Read Mark 6:45-52. Jesus had just performed the miracle of feeding the five thousand with only five loaves and two fishes. He went up to the mountain to pray and sent the disciples across the sea of Galilee.

Why did Jesus intend to pass them by (v. 48)?

Note: Jesus still intends to pass by the self-sufficient. If you want to row against the storms of life in your own strength, go ahead. He will let you until your arms fall off.

What insight should they have gained from the feeding of the 5,000?

What insight should you gain?

Why do you think their hearts were hardened?

Is yours?

Read Matthew 26:31-74. Do you think Peter was sincere in his declaration in verse 35? Why did Peter deny Jesus (see vv. 70, 72, 74)?

What do you think Peter was depending on to keep him from denying Jesus (see v. 41)?

Read Hebrews 12:26,27. Is God shaking up some things in your life? If so, what?

God is going to shake up what can and should be shaken—the created and temporal things. What is God shaking in your life that you have been depending on to overcome your addiction and find acceptance and affirmation?

As a child of God, what do you have that cannot be shaken?

If you rely on things that cannot be shaken and look to them to get your needs met, what can you look forward to?

What is God doing in your life to bring you to the point where you look only to Him for life and strength?

Read 2 Corinthians 12:7-10. How did God answer Paul's prayer?

Why didn't God answer his prayer the way Paul wanted?

Why would Paul boast about his weaknesses?

What is the qualification for having Christ's power in your life?

How have you been trying to be strong in your resources instead of depending on Christ for your strength?

Read 2 Corinthians 1:8-10. Can you relate to Paul's feelings about the hardships he suffered?

What was God's purpose for the hardships in the apostles' lives?

How have you relied on yourself instead of God who is even able to raise the dead?

What hardships are you currently going through that are putting you under great pressure?

Read Hebrews 12:4-11. What does God bring into the lives of His sons and daughters?

What is our attitude to be?

What is God's purpose in the process?

Read John 12:24-26. What comes before fruitfulness?

How do we get in the way of God's process of bringing us to the end of ourselves?

What are you holding on to and not willing to give up that is more important to you than your relationship with God?

What are you trying to gain, attain or accomplish in life that you are afraid God will not approve of or will take away if you turn everything over to Him?

Read 2 Corinthians 4:7-18. What is the treasure that you possess?

What are the earthen vessels (jars of clay in the *NIV*)?

Where do we get the power to live and overcome problems?

What does God bring into our lives to remind us where the power is?

What is the hope that we have?

What keeps us from giving up and losing heart?

What should our focus be in the midst of our troubles and trials?

Write a prayer to God. In your prayer, share with your heavenly Father what you have been relying on instead of Him. Thank Him for the hardships that have brought you to this point in your life. Tell Him that you desire to put no confidence in the flesh and that your hope is in Him. Express your decision to rely on Him for deliverance from your addiction and to meet all your needs.

D. Stating the Truth ····················

Contrary to popular belief, the addict's problem is not that he is too weak in the flesh, but that he is too strong in the flesh. We are too self-sufficient to completely give up on ourselves and our resources and throw ourselves upon the mercy of God and learn to "be strong in the Lord and in the strength of His might" (Ephesians 6:10). We believe that if we will just try a little harder, find another new program or treatment, we will be able to handle our problems. As one writer has said, "It is only when we have spent our last buck and shot our last bullet" that we are ready to completely trust God with our lives.

> **The Truth:**
> God's purpose is to bring us to the end of ourselves and
> our resources in order to discover His. Then we will trust
> Him to set us free and meet all our needs.

E. Illustrating the Truth

Read the paragraph about Jerry Clower in *Freedom from Addiction* beginning at the bottom of page 105 and continuing to the top of page 106.

How would you apply this truth to your own life?

F. Appropriating the Truth ....

In order to make the truth real and relevant to you, write out any lies robbing you of your freedom in Christ that have been exposed to you while completing this chapter. Include the lies that other group members have shared during group discussions. Then write out the truth you have learned that will help you live a free productive life in Christ. One example is given:

The Lie That Binds You	The Truth That Sets You Free
I renounce the lie that: *I need to rely on my own understanding.*	I announce the truth that: *I need to acknowledge God in all His ways.*

G. Personalizing the Truth

Internalize the truth by personalizing the Scripture and confessing it.

> Example:
> I have asked God many times to make me stronger, change my circumstances and make my problems go away, but He tells me that His grace is sufficient and wants me to depend totally on Him. I have learned that I can't do for myself what Christ has already done for me. I admit my weakness and gladly receive His power.

Personalize any Scriptures that God has revealed to you.

> Example taken from Ephesians 6:10,11:
> I will be strong in the Lord and in the strength of His might.
> I will put on the armor of God, so that I will be able to stand firm against the schemes of the devil.

Get into the habit of renouncing the lies you have believed and announcing the truth out loud and often. (If you can't do it out loud, do it in your mind.)

Reading Assignment: Chapter 9 in *Freedom from Addiction*

Understanding the Gospel and Your Heavenly Father

The Overcomer's Covenant in Christ

Statement Four

I declare the truth that I am dead to sin, freed from it and alive to God in Christ Jesus since I have died with Christ and was raised with Him. I know that the law and all my best efforts are unable to impart life, and that Jesus came to give me life.

Trying to live up to someone else's standards much less our own will prove futile. Even living in a controlled environment with external constraints will eventually prove futile. As soon as the external constraints are removed, the unregenerate man will return to his former state. Jesus didn't come to give us a new law; He came to give us life. He didn't come to change our behavior; He came to change our nature.

Every child of God is alive in Christ and dead to sin and we are to continue to believe it is so in order to live free in Christ. The law of life in Christ Jesus has set us free from the law of sin and of death (see Romans 8:2). We have become a partaker of the divine nature (see 2 Peter 1:4) because our souls are in union with Him. Human effort cannot accomplish this because we cannot do for ourselves what Christ has already done for us. Lacking this vital truth, most believers are desperately trying to become somebody they already are. "Beloved, now we are children of God" (1 John 3:2).

A. Understanding the Problem ·········

Knowing Christ and abiding in Him and His love is the key to the Christian life and victory over sin. Is your concept of God that of a loving heavenly Father who is accepting and affirming? Many see God as a harsh disciplinarian, a remote ruler, a cruel judge or worse. Such attitudes toward God will prohibit you from finding your freedom in Christ. Nobody wants to approach a vindictive God who is out to get them. Most Christians trapped in addictive behaviors see themselves as failures, and they believe God is disappointed in them and has given up on them.

Having a true knowledge of God and an understanding of who we are in Christ are the greatest determinants of the state of our mental health. A false concept of God, misplaced deification of Satan (attributing God's attributes to Satan) and ignorance of who we are in Christ are the greatest contributors to mental illness. Therefore the most effective lies that Satan uses to rob us of our freedom are related to our identity in Christ and our concept of God. Strongholds have been raised against the knowledge of God (see 2 Corinthians 10:4,5, *NIV*) and they are keeping us in bondage.

B. Making a Personal Appraisal ·········

Complete the following sentences:

When I think about God, I feel...

When I think about being alone with God, I feel...

In my relationship to God, I really desire that..

The thing that frustrates me most about God is...

Sometimes I get angry with God when...

In my experiences with God I smile when I remember...

I am usually surprised about God when He...

The person who reminds me most of God is...

The Christian who disappointed me most is...

The secret thought about God that I struggle with the most is...

If I could tell the whole world one thing about God, it would be...

The one thing I would change about myself to please God is...

Sometimes I wish God would…

The one thing I am afraid God will do is…

Look at your answers. What kind of person did you describe? Circle the word in each pair that best fits the person described in your answers above:

Insensitive	or	Compassionate
Demanding	or	Accepting
Distant	or	Intimate
Absent	or	Always there for you
Condemning	or	Forgiving
Dissatisfied with you	or	Approving and affirming
Harsh	or	Gentle
Killjoy	or	Wants you to enjoy life
Controlling	or	Gives you freedom to make choices
Accessible	or	Hard to reach

Is the person you described one you could go to with your worst problems and share your deepest secrets?

Is this the kind of person that you can intimately bond with?

Note: An unbiblical concept of God will keep you from developing an intimate relationship with Him which is essential for your freedom.

> ### The Lie:
> I can't face God because He is angry with me and has given up on me since I have failed Him so badly.

C. Discovering the Truth That Sets You Free

Remember that the key to freedom is knowing the truth. Pray the following prayer adapted from Ephesians 1:17-19 before you begin this section of discovering the truth that sets you free.

> Dear Heavenly Father,
> I ask that You would give me the Spirit of wisdom and revelation so that I may know You better. I pray also that the eyes of my heart may be enlightened in order that I may know the hope to which You have called me, the riches of Your glorious inheritance in the saints and Your incomparably great power for us who believe. In Jesus' name I pray. Amen.

Read Romans 5:6-11.

What were you like when Christ died for you?

How did God demonstrate His love to you?

What were you at the time?

List the three results (benefits) of Christ's death for us.

What was your relationship to God when Christ died for us?

Read Luke 15:1-32.

In verses 1-10, what is God's response when a person goes astray?

What happens in heaven when they are found?

In verses 11-16, how do you think the younger son was feeling?

What made him leave home?

Look at the father's response in verses 20 and 21. Why do you believe the father was able to see the son when he was a long way off?

What was the father's response to his son when he greeted him?

Why do you think the father didn't let the son finish his speech?

What did the son have to do to get back into the father's good graces?

Did the father treat the son like a second-class citizen, a wayward son who had messed up and was no longer worthy of his father's love?

Why would the father treat his wayward son this way (see Ephesians 2:7-9)?

Note: God is not a codependent or an enabler. An often overlooked message of this parable is that the father let him leave so he could experience the consequences of his ungodly, sinful and irresponsible behavior.

Read Romans 4:7,8.

What has God done about all your sins—past, present and future?

Once you have confessed your sins to God, will He bring them up to you again (see Psalm 103:12)?

Who is the accuser of the brethren who will remind you of every sin you ever committed (see Revelation 12:10)?

Read Romans 4:25—5:1.

Because of Christ's death, how is our relationship with God characterized now?

What position do we have with God right now (i.e. what is our standing with Him)?

Because of what God has done and where He has placed us, what should our response be when things don't go the way we want?

Why shouldn't we be disappointed?

How much are you worth—what value does God place on you?

If you asked God what you were worth, what would He say?

Note: The worth of something is determined by what someone is willing to pay for it.

Read 1 Timothy 2:5,6 and Titus 2:14

What did God have to give for you?

What are you worth in the eyes of God—your real worth, regardless of how you feel?

Read Psalm 23.

If God is your Shepherd, what do you lack (v. 1)?

What does "He makes me lie down in green pastures" (v. 2) mean to you?

When and where do you need to be led "beside quiet waters" (v. 2)?

How does your soul need restoring (v. 3)?

Where do you need His guidance (v. 3)?

In what valleys do you need to feel His presence (v. 4)?

What fears do you need to give over to Him (v. 4)?

What enemies do you need protection from (v. 5)?

In what ways do you need to be comforted (v. 5)?

In what ways have you experienced the overflowing abundance He offers you (v. 5)?

What tough situations are you facing for which you need God's supernatural enabling?

According to this psalm, can you depend on God for the rest of your life?

Read Psalm 103.

What are God's benefits to you listed in verses 1-7?

In verses 8-14, how does God relate to us?

Do you think a person with these attributes could understand you and your problems?

Read Matthew 9:36.

How did Jesus respond to those who were distressed and downcast?

Read Matthew 11:28-30.

Who is Jesus giving His invitation to?

What does He offer you?

If you are not experiencing what Jesus offers, have you perhaps been looking in the wrong place for help and comfort?

How does He describe Himself?

Is this the kind of person you could go to with your problems? Why or why not?

Read John 15:1-9.

Jesus says our heavenly Father is glorified if we bear fruit. What is the difference between bearing fruit and abiding in Christ?

What is *our* responsibility—bearing fruit or abiding in Christ (v. 4)? What is *Christ's* responsibility?

How much does Jesus say He loves you (v. 9)?

What should your response to His love be (v. 9)?

When and where are you most likely not to abide in (remain in, stay in, or rely on) Jesus' love? Are your real needs getting met, and are you bearing fruit during those times and places you are not abiding?

Note: A working definition of insanity is "continuing to do the same things, but expecting different results."

D. Stating the Truth

> **The Truth:**
> God's love for me is unconditional because He is
> love. There is nothing that I can do to make Him
> love me more. There is nothing that I can do to
> make Him love me less.

Record any truth that you have learned by yourself or from the group
that you need to incorporate into your life.

E. Illustrating the Truth

Read pages 100-101 in *Freedom from Addiction* beginning with "One
afternoon..." and ending with "...these words rang true." How does
this testimony relate to you?

F. Appropriating the Truth

In order to make the truth real and relevant to you, write out the lies you have been believing that have been exposed during your preparation and during your group session. Then write out the truth you have learned that will set you free. Examples are given:

The Lie That Binds You	The Truth That Sets You Free
I renounce the lie that my Heavenly Father is: *Distant and disinterested.* *Insensitive and uncaring.* *Stern or demanding.* *Passive and cold.* *Absent.* *Dissatisfied with me.* *Harsh.* *A killjoy.* *Controlling and manipulative.* *Condemning or unforgiving.*	I announce the truth that my Heavenly Father is: *Intimate and involved.* *Kind and compassionate.* *Accepting and loving.* *Warm and affectionate.* *Always with me.* *Approving and affirming.* *Gentle and protective of me.* *Came to give me abundant life.* *Full of grace and mercy.* *Tenderhearted and forgiving.*

In the chart above, list other lies that you have believed and the truth that you have learned.

G. Personalizing the Truth ··········

Internalize the truth by personalizing the Scripture and confessing it.

Example:
When I sin and rebel against God, He still loves me and eagerly awaits my return. When I come to my senses and return He welcomes me and embraces me with love and compassion. He receives me as His dearly loved child and He rejoices, celebrates and favors me with His blessings.

Personalize any Scriptures that God has revealed to you.

Example from 1 John 4:16:
I have come to know and have believed the love which God has for me. God is love, and I choose to abide in His love. I abide in God's love, and He abides in me.

Stay in the habit of renouncing the lies you have believed and announcing the truth out loud and often. (If you can't do it out loud, do it in your mind.)

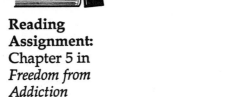
Our Identity in Christ

··

The Overcomer's Covenant in Christ

── Statement Five ──

I gladly embrace the truth that I am now a child of God who is unconditionally loved and accepted. I reject the lie that I have to perform to be accepted. I also reject my fallen and natural identity which was derived from the world. I know that it is not what I do that determines who I am, but who I am that determines what I do.

We are not alcoholics, addicts or codependents. We are children of God who are trusting in Christ to be our lives and our freedom. Rehearsing a fallen identity may reinforce the lie that we have to sin. We are children of God who struggle to overcome the temptations of alcohol, sex, drugs, or the many other sins that so easily beset us. We are not sinners in the hands of an angry God. We are saints in the hands of a loving God. We can do all things through Christ who strengthens us (see Philippians 4:13).

······· A. Understanding the Problem

In the last chapter we shared that the most effective lies that Satan uses to keep you in bondage concern your identity in Christ, who God is and your relationship with Him. In this section we will look at the truth about who you are in Christ and expose the lies of the one who accuses the brethren day and night. The general tendency of fallen humanity is for men to get their identity from their careers and for women to get their identity from having and raising a family. With the disintegration of the nuclear family at the end of the twentieth century, many women have come to find their identity in their careers as well. The point is that people have a tendency to get their identity from the things they do.

A booth in a mall was selling T-shirts with the following logos: "Hunting Is My Life," "Fishing Is My Life," "Hiking Is My Life," "Softball Is My Life," etc. Hunting? Fishing? Hiking? Softball? The apostle Paul would likely have said, "Get a life!" He actually did say "For to me, to live is Christ, and to die is gain" (Philippians 1:21).

Try putting anything else in that statement. "For to me, to live is (my career, studies, family, spouse, children, money, possessions, ministry), and to die would be loss." The problem with putting any other value, pleasure or pursuit (including softball) in the statement is that you could lose any of those things at anytime or never gain it at all. A would-be Olympic gymnast at the national trials said, "Every day since I was five years old, I have thought about nothing else but making the Olympic team. It is all I want. It is my life." Unfortunately he *didn't* make the team.

B. Making a Personal Appraisal

Write a paragraph of introduction about yourself, describing who you are to someone you have never met.

Give a short description of who the following people are:

Bill Clinton:

Michael Jordan:

Babe Ruth:

Madonna:

Billy Graham:

Paul Newman:

Mother Teresa:

What was the first thing that came to your mind when you saw those names? Chances are it was what they did professionally. Did the thought even cross your mind that they were someone created in the image of God or that they were somebody's child, parent or friend? We have been conditioned to identify people and ourselves by what we do. What did Paul mean when he wrote, "Therefore from now on we recognize no [one] according to the flesh" (2 Corinthians 5:16)?

How important to your sense of worth is your...

Appearance?

Performance?

Social status?

Education?

Who would you be and how would it affect your self-perception if something happened to destroy your appearance, social status or your ability to perform? Could that happen?

Think of one person you admire the most. What is it about that person that you admire (i.e. their appearance, performance, status, character, etc.)?

Generally speaking, what do people look up to and admire most in others: their appearance, performance, status or their character?

How have your past failures affected the way you perceive yourself and your sense of worth?

Do you think you are an alcoholic, addict, compulsive gambler, adult child of an alcoholic, anorexic, bulimic, sex addict, etc. because of your struggle with addiction? Why or why not?

Are you trying to change your behavior hoping that it will change you as a person?

Can you change who you are by how you behave? How?

How well and how long would you have to behave a certain way in order to change who you are?

What if you failed? Would you have to start over again?

Mark each statement either *T* for true or *F* for false:

_____ Once an addict always an addict.

_____ The best I can hope for is to control my problem.

_____ I was born with my addiction so I will always have it.

_____ My addiction is part of me.

_____ I cannot think about who I really am apart from my addiction.

_____ I could never do what it would take to be free.

_____ My addiction is something I will have to live with the rest of my life.

_____ I'm different from others and my problem is different.

_____ I have gone too far to be free.

_____ I am not morally good enough to do right and be free.

_____ My addiction is too strong for me to overcome.

_____ That's just the way I am. I really don't have a choice.

_____ My background and my environment conditioned me, and I'm trapped.

_____ I'm being punished for the bad life I've lived.

_____ I just don't believe that freedom from addiction is a possibility.

If you answered true to any of the above you have been deceived and with such beliefs you will likely continue to struggle with your addiction. God has not equally distributed gifts, talents nor intelligence. Many are born into oppressive social situations and some are less attractive than others. Can those who seemed to have gotten the short end of the stick have any hope for happiness, success, fulfillment or any legitimate sense of worth? How?

Who or what is the great equalizer?

When you were growing up did you have a dream, a goal or an ideal of who you wanted to be and how you wanted life to turn out? Write a short paragraph describing what you hoped for.

On a separate piece of paper write a short letter to your father. Tell him what you would have liked to have gotten from him that you didn't get while growing up. Tell him what you would have liked for him to be and to do with you, or for you, etc. **Don't mail the letter. This is for your benefit only.**

On a separate piece of paper write a short letter to your mother. Tell her what you would have liked to have gotten from her that you didn't get while growing up. Tell her what you would have liked for her to be or to do with you, or for you, etc. **Don't mail the letter. This is for your benefit only.**

If you could change your childhood, what would you change about it?

How would you have liked your childhood to be different?

What we missed in childhood may become the driving force for the rest of our life. The girl who never got approval from her dad is driven to try to get acceptance from men. The boy whose dad never gave him approval becomes a workaholic seeking to prove he is okay. Do you see such a pattern in your life?

What do you think has been the driving force in your life?

How and where have you tried to find acceptance, security and significance?

How have you tried to prove to yourself or someone else that you are okay, acceptable, worthy, lovable, etc.?

No matter how hard we try, every attempt at self-verification will crumble under hostile rejection or angry criticism. It is futile to play for the grandstand when we have been called to play for the Coach. Even the most legendary human coaches have had their critics. Even if you lived a perfect life, someone would object. There was only One who lived a perfect life and nearly everyone called for His crucifixion. Like Christ, we are "rejected by men, but choice and precious in the sight of God" (1 Peter 2:4). Success is accepting God's goals for our lives and by His grace becoming what He has called us to be. Nobody can block that goal for our lives except ourselves.

> **The Lie:**
> Who I am is determined by what I do and since I am
> just a product of my past I am therefore an
> addict who will never change.

C. Discovering the Truth That Sets You Free

Remember that the key to freedom is knowing the truth. Pray the following prayer adapted from Ephesians 1:17-19 before you begin this section of discovering the truth that sets you free:

> Dear Heavenly Father,
> I will continue to ask that You would give me the Spirit of wisdom and revelation, so that I may know You better. I also pray that the eyes of my heart may be enlightened in order that I may know the hope to which You have called me, the riches of Your glorious inheritance in the saints and Your incomparably great power for us who believe. In Jesus' name, I pray. Amen.

Read 1 John 3:1-3.

Who does God say you are?

Do you have to purify yourself in order to be a child of God, or does knowing who you are affect how you live? Explain.

How would this truth affect recovery ministries?

Read Galatians 4:4-7.

What is different about you now that you are a child of God?

Knowing that, how should you respond to God?

Read Romans 8:15,16. What two major problems of life does God provide an answer for when we become children of God?

Read John 14:20. What two things do we need to realize about ourselves that will greatly affect our self-perception?

Read 2 Corinthians 5:17. What has changed now that you have become a Christian?

Read Galatians 3:26-29. What is your relationship to Christ now?

Read 2 Peter 1:4. What has God given you to enable you to overcome your addiction?

Read Galatians 2:20.

What or who is your life now?

How do you live it?

Whose life is it that enables you to live by faith?

Note: It is really both your life *and* Christ's life. God never designed mankind to live separate from Him. Adam and Eve were created both physically and spiritually alive. What Adam and Eve lost when they sinned was spiritual life, i.e. their souls were no longer in union with God. What Jesus came to do was give us life (see John 10:10). Those who are born again are now spiritually alive. "For you have died [to who you were before] and your life is hidden with Christ in God" (Colossians 3:3).
Read Ephesians 1:1-14.

How did Paul identify the Ephesian Christians (v. 1)?

What have we received from God (v. 2)?

What has He blessed us with (v. 3)?

What did He choose us to be (v. 4)?

Who are we (v. 5)?

What does He freely give us (v. 6)?

What do we have as a result of the riches of His grace (v. 7)?

What has He poured out on us (vv. 7,8)?

What does He make known to us (v. 9)?

Under whom will He bring all things together (v. 10)?

What has happened to us as a result of His plan (v. 11)?

What was the purpose of His plan (v. 12)?

Where are we placed when we hear the gospel and believe it (v. 13)?

What are we guaranteed (v. 14)?

Read 1 Peter 2:9,10. How have your credentials improved without you having to do anything?

Read 1 Corinthians 6:9-11. What three things have happened to you?

Note: In this passage "washed" means "to be regenerated." Salvation is not adding something new to who we already are; it is a transformation where we have put off the old self and put on the new self. In being born again we become new creations in Christ. Justified means that we have been fully forgiven of our sins and given a right standing before God. Sanctified means to be set apart by God as saints who are now in Christ and being perfected as He is holy. See *The Common Made Holy* by Dr. Neil Anderson and Dr. Robert Saucy (Harvest House) for a comprehensive teaching on how God transforms us from sinners to saints and how we can conform to the image of God.

Who are you? Are you what people say about you? Are you what you believe about yourself? Or are you what God says about you? Who does God say you are? Look up the verses below and write out who God says you are.

God's Word says I am...

Matthew 5:13

Matthew 5:14

John 1:12

John 15:1,5

John 15:8

John 15:15

Acts 1:8

Romans 6:18

Romans 8:14,15

Romans 8:17

Romans 8:33,34

Romans 8:35

1 Corinthians 3:16

1 Corinthians 6:17

1 Corinthians 12:27

2 Corinthians 1:21

2 Corinthians 5:17

2 Corinthians 6:1

Ephesians 2:10

Colossians 3:3

1 Peter 2:5

1 Peter 2:9,10

1 John 5:18

Note: Billy Graham said, "God said it, I believe it and that settles it." No matter what anyone else says or what I feel, I am who God says I am. I may not feel like or sometimes act like it and others may disagree, but that is who I really am.

D. Stating the Truth

It is absolutely essential for you to understand who you are in Christ if you ever hope to live a free and productive life. No one can consistently behave in a way that is inconsistent with how he or she perceives him- or herself. The problem is not what you are doing, the problem is what you are believing. Your behavior is just an expression of what you are choosing to believe. The answer is not in what you do, but what God has already done for you which you can only appropriate by faith. A person who understands who he or she is in Christ and walks by faith, according to what God says is true, will not engage in self-destructive behavior.

> **The Truth:**
> It is not what I do that determines who I am. It is who I am that determines what I do. I am a child of God and I am alive in Christ. I am not an addict. I am a new creation in Christ who is forgiven, cleansed and justified before God.

Record any truth that you have learned in this chapter.

E. Illustrating the Truth ·············

Read pages 123-125 in *Freedom from Addiction* beginning with "On October 24, I got drunk again…" and ending with "…Praise God I was free at last!" How does this testimony personally relate to you?

F. Appropriating the Truth ·············

List other lies that you have believed and the truth that you have learned:

The Lie That Binds You	The Truth That Sets You Free
I renounce the lie that: *What I do determines who I am.* *I'm a sinner.* *I'm an addict*	I announce the truth that: *Who I am determines what I do.* *I'm a saint who sins.* *I'm a child of God who struggles with* _____ .

G. Personalizing the Truth

Internalize the truth by personalizing Scripture and confessing it. Record insights that you have gotten from other members in the group.

> Example using 1 John 3:1-3:
> See how great a love my Father has bestowed on me that I should be called a child of God and that is who I am. For this reason the world does not know who I really am because they don't know God. Now I am a child of God, and I don't fully know what I will be. I do know that when Jesus comes back that I shall be like Him because I will see Him just as He really is. As long as I have my hope fixed on Him I will purify myself.

Get into the habit of renouncing the lies you have believed and announcing the truth out loud and often. (If you can't do it out loud, do it in your mind.)

Freedom from Fear

Reading Assignment:
Chapter 6 in
Freedom from Addiction

....

The Overcomer's Covenant in Christ

Statement Six

I declare that sin shall no longer be master over me because I am not under the law, but under grace and there is no more guilt or condemnation because I am spiritually alive in Christ Jesus. I am a servant of a new covenant, not of the letter, but of the Spirit; for the letter kills, but the Spirit gives life.

Every child of God has been transferred out of the kingdom of darkness into the kingdom of the Lord Jesus Christ (see Colossians 1:13). We are no longer dead in our trespasses and sins (see Ephesians 2:1). We consider ourselves to be alive to Christ and dead to sin (see Romans 6:11). We don't make that true by our experiences. We choose to believe what God says is true and walk accordingly by faith, and then it works out in our experiences. We don't try to live a victorious and fruitful life with the hope that God may someday love and accept us. God already loves and accepts us, and that is why we live a fruitful and victorious life by the grace of God.

We no longer attempt to live only on the basis of laws and principles which call for us to respond in obedience. We have died and our lives are hidden with Christ in God (see Colossians 3:3). We respond to the life of Christ within us by faith according to what God says is true. We walk (live) by the Spirit and do not carry out the desires of the flesh (see Galatians 5:16).

Paul says, "Not that we are adequate in ourselves to consider anything as coming from ourselves, but our adequacy is from God, who also made us adequate as servants of a new covenant, not of the letter, but of the Spirit; for the letter kills, but the Spirit gives life" (2 Corinthians 3:5,6).

·········· A. Understanding the Problem

Anxiety is a fear of the unknown or fear without an adequate cause. The basis for anxiety is uncertainty and a lack of trust. According to Scripture, we worry about what we treasure in our hearts (see Matthew 6:19-24), and we worry about tomorrow (see vv. 25-34), because we don't know what will happen. Jesus says, "Do not be anxious for tomorrow" (v. 34), because your heavenly Father will take care of you.

To be anxious is to be double minded. That is why Jesus said, "No one can serve two masters; for either he will hate the one and love the other, or he will hold to one and despise the other. You cannot serve God and mammon. For this reason I say to you, do not be anxious for your life" (Matthew 6:24,25). A mind that is free and pure has a single focus.

James wrote that if we are experiencing trials in life, we should ask the Lord in faith for wisdom. But if we are overcome by doubting thoughts, we will be overcome by the storms of life. "Let not that man expect that he will receive anything from the Lord, being a double-minded man, unstable in all his ways" (James 1:7,8). God is the antidote for anxiety. Therefore, cast "all your anxiety upon Him, because He cares for you" (1 Peter 5:7). We have to choose to trust Him and turn to Him in prayer. "Be anxious for nothing, but in everything by prayer and supplication with thanksgiving let your requests be made known to God" (Philippians 4:6).

Unlike anxiety, fear has an object. Fears are even categorized by their objects. For instance, claustrophobia is a fear of closed places. Xenophobia is a fear of strangers or foreigners. Agoraphobia is a generalized fear of public places where people seem to close in on us. In order for a fear object to be legitimate it must have two attributes: It must be perceived as potent (having power) and it must be imminent (present).

For instance, having been a diver and rescue swimmer in the Navy,

I (Neil) have what I think is a healthy fear of sharks. But as I am writing this, I sense no fear of them at all because there are none in the room. If I were to jump into a pool full of sharks, I would probably set some speed records for swimming. I would have an immediate fear response because sharks are now both imminent and potent in my mind. If I didn't see the sharks, I wouldn't be afraid either, even though I should be. Neither would I be afraid if the sharks in the pool were dead—provided I was sure they were dead!

All you have to do to eliminate a fear object is to remove just one of its attributes. For instance, death is no longer a legitimate fear object for us because God has removed one of the attributes. Although death is still imminent, it is no longer potent because "death is swallowed up in victory" (1 Corinthians 15:54). Therefore Paul could write, "For to me, to live is Christ, and to die is gain" (Philippians 1:21). Some would believe that the worst thing that could happen to them is to die, but physical death is not the ultimate value. You would just be in the presence of your heavenly Father and in far better shape than you are now. Spiritual life is the ultimate value. It will be heaven when our souls separate from our bodies; it will be hell if our souls are separated from God. "And do not fear those who kill the body, but are unable to kill the soul; but rather fear Him who is able to destroy both soul and body in hell" (Matthew 10:28).

That is not a license to commit suicide nor an excuse not to be a good steward of the physical life that God has given to us. It is a liberating truth, however. The one who is free from the fear of death is free to live in a responsible way. We are also not to fear mankind. "Even if you should suffer for the sake of righteousness, you are blessed. And do not fear their intimidation, and do not be troubled, but sanctify Christ as Lord in your hearts, always being ready to make a defense to everyone who asks you to give an account for the hope that is in you, yet with gentleness and reverence" (1 Peter 3:14,15).

Why is "the fear of the Lord...the beginning of wisdom" (Proverbs 9:10)? Because the fear of the Lord is the one fear that expels all other fears. What two attributes of God make Him the ultimate object of fear? He is omnipotent (all powerful), and omnipresent (everywhere present). We don't worship God because He needs His ego stroked, and He doesn't need you and I to tell Him who He is. God is totally sufficient in and of Himself. We worship God because we need to keep His divine attributes constantly before us.

When I (Neil) have asked Christian congregations all over the world if they have had a fearful encounter with some spiritual force that frightened them, at least 50 percent have responded affirmatively. I have found it to be higher among Christian leaders, which shouldn't surprise us. At least 35 percent of the same audiences have awakened either terrorized or alertly awake at a precise time in the morning such as 3:00 A.M. Such a terror attack may feel as though you have a pressure on your chest or something grabbing your throat. When you try to respond physically, it may appear as though you can't. You want to call upon the Lord, but you can't even say the name "Jesus." Why not?

Because "The weapons of our warfare are not of the flesh, but divinely powerful for the destruction of fortresses" (2 Corinthians 10:4). Trying to physically respond may prove fruitless. Since God is "able to judge the thoughts and intentions of the heart" (Hebrews 4:12), we can always call upon Him in our hearts and minds. As soon as we acknowledge Him and His authority in the inner person, we will be free to call upon the name of the Lord by verbally saying "Jesus." That is all you have to say and do. James says that if you submit to God and then resist the devil, he will flee from you (see v. 4:7), but you'd better do it in that order.

Please don't assume that every time you awake in the middle of the night it is a spiritual attack. In most cases you probably need to go to the bathroom or your stomach is not reacting very well to the pickle you ate. But if a definite pattern exists such as the awakening being abrupt and at a certain time rather than a gradual awareness that is more natural, then it could be a spiritual attack. You could also be rudely awakened by a burglar trying to enter your house or a gust of wind that causes a shutter to bang.

I (Neil) am not a timid person, but I have felt the terror of a spiritual attack at night. In each case, I have experienced immediate victory by turning to God in the inner man, and then verbally resisting the devil. If the attacks persist, it is probably because of some unresolved issues either in your life or in your home.

Panic attacks may also occur during the day. Usually they can be traced to deceiving thoughts. Have you ever been driving your car and then suddenly become overwhelmed by impulsive thoughts such as, *Drive into that car beside you* or *Jump out of the car*. Have you ever felt panic stricken as you looked over a cliff and thought, *Jump!*

Many people who struggle with agoraphobia have mitral valve prolapse. It usually is not a serious condition of the heart, but it does cause the heart to flutter, often causing the person to panic. They don't want to panic in a social setting so they begin to do things to avoid having a reaction in public. The most common remedy is to stay at home, but that is not what the Lord would have you do. You are letting that fear control your life. This kind of fear needs to be faced and overcome.

People struggling with addictive behaviors have all kinds of bizarre thoughts and hallucinations. They see and hear many frightening things. That kind of attack on the mind by the accuser of the brethren has left many people questioning their salvation or becoming paralyzed with fear. If you shared some of these experiences with a secular doctor or counselor, they would call it an anxiety or a panic attack. They should call it a fear attack because that is what it really is. They call it an anxiety or panic attack because they can't identify the fear object. Therefore, it would better fall under the definition of anxiety. I can identify the object of their fear, however, and so should you. Every child of God should be taught to discern a spiritual attack and how to resolve it.

There is a major difference between fears that are developed over time and those that are essentially attacks. The latter must be dealt with at the time. When people hear or see something that frightens them and they discern that it is a spiritual attack, they can exercise their authority in Christ by submitting to Him and resisting the devil. Taking our place in Christ may require us to verbally express that we are children of God and the evil one cannot touch us (see 1 John 5:18). This requires some discernment, however. If you are being harassed or attacked by another person, that person might not necessarily be under the influence of demons. He or she might be under the influence of drugs or alcohol, or perhaps experiencing a mental or social problem. In that case you may need to take steps to protect yourself and others from physical harm.

Irrational fears that are learned over time must be unlearned and that will take time. First, you have to separate legitimate fears which are necessary for survival from irrational fears, or phobias. Phobias either compel us to do something that is irresponsible or prevent us from doing that which is responsible. We will give you an opportunity to analyze your fears later on in this chapter.

Fear is a crippler. You cannot walk in freedom if you fear anything other than God. You cannot walk by faith if fear is controlling your life. Fear of anything other than God is mutually exclusive of faith in God. He is the only legitimate fear object. Yet many Christians are bound by fear. If we understood our position and authority in Christ and God's unfailing love and protection, we would never have to be fearful again. Not that we would never have feelings of fear, but such feelings should not have any control over our lives nor determine how we behave. The psalmist said, "When I am afraid, I will put my trust in Thee" (Psalm 56:3). He made a conscious choice of his will to turn to the Lord and trust Him.

Fear and bondage go hand in hand. The addict is afraid he will never change, fearful of what it would be like if he did change, worried about losing what he treasures most, fearful of what others think and most afraid of the dreadful crisis that every addict believes he is relentlessly moving toward.

Fear is one of Satan's greatest weapons. He wants to be worshiped by deceiving us into thinking that he is the ultimate fear object. Those who are afraid of the devil and his demons have no fear of God. That fear is just the opposite of what Scripture teaches. There isn't a verse in the Bible that indicates we should fear Satan. There are over 100 references in the Bible that say "Fear not" or "Don't be afraid."

[B] B. Making a Personal Appraisal

Number up to five of the following fears with which you have struggled in order of the greatest to the least (5 being the greatest, 1 being the least):

___ Losing control   ___ Inability to change   ___ Death of a spouse
___ Being alone   ___ Humiliation   ___ Loss of reputation
___ Death   ___ Losing your mind   ___ Losing good health
___ Failure   ___ Being homeless   ___ Rejection
___ Loss of a job   ___ Darkness   ___ Being institutionalized

___ Other _____

What do you fear that you might lose?

Making God the ultimate fear object in your life, as opposed to Satan, humankind or death, will greatly affect our attitudes about life as the following chart illustrates. Add some of your own attitudes:

If we believe God is all powerful and omnipresent our attitudes will be:	If we allow Satan, man or death to be legitimate fear objects our attitudes will be:
Thankful for all God has done.	*Complaining, doubting God's provision.*
Peaceful, trusting in God.	*Anxious, doubting that God cares.*
Content, knowing God is enough.	*Discontent, questioning God's sufficiency.*
Encouraged in the Lord.	*Discouraged by my enemies.*
Confident in Christ.	*Fearful of illegitimate fear objects.*
Joyful in the Lord.	*Depressed by life's circumstances.*

What is the lie that keeps us in bondage because of fear and anxiety? Basically the lie boils down to the belief that "God is unable or unwilling to help me in my circumstances because He really isn't omnipotent, omnipresent and all-loving." If you continue to believe that, you will continue to live in fear and bondage.

> **The Lie:**
> God doesn't care about me or my situation and is unwilling or unable to do anything about it. I am at the mercy of Satan, humankind and negative circumstances. So I live in fear of the future.

C. Discovering the Truth That Sets You Free

Remember that the key to freedom is knowing the truth. Pray the following prayer adapted from Ephesians 1:17-19 before you begin this section of discovering the truth that sets you free:

Dear Heavenly Father,
I continue to ask that You give me the Spirit of wisdom and revelation so that I may know You better. I pray that the eyes of my heart may be enlightened in order that I may know the hope to which You have called me, the riches of Your glorious inheritance in the saints and Your incomparably great power for us who believe. In Jesus' name, I pray. Amen.

Read 1 John 4:13-18.

What do you have that should enable you not to be fearful?

When you become fearful and anxious, you have lost your focus and are not relying on God. "For God has not given us a spirit of timidity, but of power and love and discipline" (2 Timothy 1:7). When you think of your biggest problem or greatest fear, what is your focus?

What enables you to be confident of the future?

When you become fearful and anxious, what are you doubting about God?

If fear has to do with torment (punishment), who do you think is the author of fear?

Read Philippians 4:6,7.

What are you to do about things that trouble you?

What should your attitude be in prayer?

What is the result of this attitude?

Would that leave any place for fear?

What have you been anxious about that you haven't prayerfully submitted to God?

Read 1 Peter 5:7.

Someone said that every decision is made in an attempt to minimize future anxiety or presently reduce it. Can you see how your addictive behavior has been an attempt to cover up fears and anxieties? Explain.

Does the bartender, the dope dealer, smut peddler or any other enabler care for you?

Such temporary cures for anxiety only produce greater anxiety the next day when the effects of the temporary cure wear off. How can you cast all your anxiety onto Christ? Refer back to the list you made of your greatest fears and anxieties.

Read John 16:33, Romans 8:15 and 2 Timothy 1:7. What three things has God done so that you don't have to live in fear?

Read Mark 4:35-41.

What did Jesus tell the disciples that if they remembered would have kept them from being afraid?

What two major concerns or fears do people have about their situation that Jesus addresses in this passage (see vv. 38,39)?

Read Psalm 121.

Where was the psalmist looking for help (v. 1)?

In what ways does the psalmist describe God that encourage you that He is able to take care of you?

Read Romans 8:28-39.

What has God promised to do no matter what comes into our lives (v. 39)?

What are the four things that God has done to make sure we are going to turn out the way He wants?

Who or what can stop you from being the person God wants you to be?

How has God proved that He loves and cares for you and has your best interest at heart?

Who is the one that will condemn you by bringing charges against you, or trying to separate you from the love of Christ?

In all your troubles, pitfalls, setbacks and the opposition against you, what is God's plan for you in all of this? Check one of the following:
- ❑ Make it through by the skin of your teeth.
- ❑ Grin and bear it.
- ❑ Keep a stiff upper lip.
- ❑ Resignation
- ❑ Victory

Read Colossians 2:15 and 1 John 5:18. Why doesn't a Christian have to fear Satan?

Read Ephesians 1:18,19; 3:20; 6:10-13 and Colossians 1:29. According to Paul, what is the source of our strength and power in the spiritual realm?

Read Ephesians 2:4-7.

What were God's two reasons for making you alive with Christ when you were dead in your sins (v. 4)?

What was God's purpose for raising you from the dead and seating you with Christ in the heavenlies?

Note: The authority you have in Christ is actually His authority to rule over the kingdom of darkness. You share it because of your position in Christ and in order to carry on the work of Christ while you are on planet Earth. You don't have the authority to do whatever you want to do. You only have the authority to do God's will.
Read 1 Peter 3:13-15.

What are we to do so that we will not fear what unbelievers fear (v. 14)?

Is there any fear object or anxious situation that lies beyond the scope of God's power and authority?

Read Psalm 118:5,6. Why do we not need to fear people?

Read Mark 5:21-43.

When the men came from Jairus's house and told him that his daughter was dead, how do you suppose he felt?

How would you have felt?

What situation do you have in your life that appears to be humanly hopeless? As good as dead? It's over? Too late?

When they told Jairus she was dead, what did Jesus say to Jairus?

If Jairus had looked at the circumstances from a human perspective with finite resources, what do you think his response would have been?

It is not the circumstances of life that determine our responses but our perspective of them. We can respond in faith, trusting "that God causes all things to work together for good to those who love God, to those who are called according to His purpose" (Romans 8:28). How does Jesus show us in this story about Jairus that He truly cares and is able to help?

In Mark 5:36, "Jesus said, 'Do not be afraid any longer, only believe '" To respond in faith, you may have to ignore your feelings, your life's circumstances and what others say. Truth is truth whether we believe it or not, but it is only effective to the degree that you choose to live by it. The key to victorious Christian living is to act on the basis of what God says is true regardless of your feelings.

D. Stating the Truth

If we are fearful and anxious, it is because we have chosen to focus on the problem instead of the solution. God is the only legitimate fear object and we can cast our anxieties onto Him because He cares for us. Those who are free in Christ don't fear death nor do they have to worry about tomorrow. God is in charge, and all the benefits of knowing that will be sensed in our spirit if we will only trust in Him. He is the blessed controller of all things.

> **The Truth:**
> God is the only legitimate omnipotent and omnipresent fear object, and He cares for us. Satan, death and humankind are illegitimate fear objects. By faith I can choose to cast all my cares upon Christ and not worry about tomorrow.

Record any new truths you have learned.

E. Illustrating the Truth

Read pages 158-160 in *Freedom from Addiction*, beginning with "Last year I got a personal reminder of this truth..." and ending with "We are free to rest in Christ." How does this relate to you?

F. Appropriating the Truth

Analyzing Your Fear

We are going to depart from our normal procedure in this chapter and give you two exercises to help you analyze your fears and anxieties. Understand that we don't fear God because of the possibility of punishment. "There is no fear in love; but perfect love casts out fear, because fear involves punishment, and the one who fears is not perfected in love" (1 John 4:18). When we make God the ultimate fear object then He becomes our sanctuary. Read the words of Isaiah 8:12-14, "You are not to fear what they fear or be in dread of it. It is the LORD of hosts whom you should regard as holy. And He shall be your fear, and He shall be your dread. Then He shall become a sanctuary."

Refer to the "Phobia Finder" on page 133 to help you analyze and eliminate any learned phobias. First, analyze your fear. Identify all fear objects. What is it you're afraid of? A problem well stated is half solved. Most people aren't always aware of what's controlling their lives. Remember, "God has not given us a spirit of timidity, but of power and love and discipline" (2 Timothy 1:7).

If you are struggling with anxiety attacks, determine when they first occurred. What experience preceded the first attack? People struggling with agoraphobia can usually identify one precipitating event. It is often associated with some tragedy or failure in their lives. Satan takes advantage of victimized people if they don't seek a scriptural solution in their crisis. Affairs and abortions have often preceded anxiety attacks. The psalmist wrote, "For I confess my iniquity; I am full of anxiety because of my sin" (Psalm 38:18). Hopefully you dealt with that when you went through the Steps to Freedom in Christ. If not, go back and repeat Step Six which will help you repent of these sins.

Second, determine where God's place in your life has been usurped. In what way does fear prevent you from responsible behavior or compel you toward irresponsible behavior? You may need to confess any active or passive participation where you've allowed fear to control your life. "The wicked flee when no one is pursuing, but the righteous are bold as a lion" (Proverbs 28:1). We will always live less than a responsible life if we fear anything other than God. Sanctify Christ as the Lord of your life. Make God your sanctuary and commit yourself to live a responsible life according to His will.

Third, work out a plan of responsible behavior. A college girl shared with me that she was living in terror of her father. They hadn't spoken to each other in six months. Obviously there was irresponsible behavior on both sides. I asked her what she would be afraid of if she went home and assumed her responsibility as her father's daughter. I suggested that evening she could take the initiative and say, "Hi, Dad!" We reasoned that there were three possible responses he could have. First, he could get mad. Second, he could respond with a greeting. Third, he could remain silent. It was the possibility of this last response that created the most fear.

We determined in advance what her response would be in each of those three cases. That's the fourth point in the phobia finder.

Determine in advance what your responses will be to every possible situation. Finally, I asked her if she would be willing to commit herself to carry out her plan. She agreed to do it. I got a call that evening from a happy girl who exclaimed, "He said 'Hi' back!" Do the thing you fear the most, and the death of fear is certain. Listen to the words of Psalm 91:1-5,9,10:

> He who dwells in the shelter of the Most High will abide in the shadow of the Almighty. I will say to the LORD, "My refuge and my fortress, my God, in whom I trust!" For it is He who delivers you from the snare of the trapper, and from the deadly pestilence. He will cover you with His pinions, and under His wings you may seek refuge; His faithfulness is a shield and bulwark. You will not be afraid of the terror by night, or of the arrow that flies by day. For you have made the LORD, my refuge, even the Most High, your dwelling place. No evil will befall you, nor will any plague come near your tent.

Phobia Finder

1. Analyze Your Fear

a. What are you afraid of? Identify *all* of your fear objects.

b. When did you first experience the fear or anxiety attack?

c. What events preceded the first occurrence?

2. Determine where God's place in your life has been usurped.

a. In what way does any fear...
Prevent you from behaving responsibly?

Compel you toward behaving irresponsibly?

b. Confess any active or passive participation on your part where you have allowed fear to control your life.

c. Commit yourself to God with the understanding that you are willing to fulfill your responsibility in the matter.

3. Work out a plan of responsible behavior.

4. Determine in advance what your response will be to every possible reaction.

5. Commit yourself to carrying out the plan.

Analyzing Your Anxiety

To be in the will of God you must live responsibly today and trust Him for tomorrow. Are you a person of little faith, or do you really believe that the fruit of the Spirit will satisfy you more than earthly possessions? Do you really believe that if you hunger and thirst after righteousness, you shall be satisfied (see Matthew 5:6)? Do you really believe that if you seek to establish God's kingdom that God will supply all your needs according to His riches in glory? If you do, then you will "seek first His kingdom and His righteousness, and all these things shall be added to you" (Matthew 6:33).

Let's assume that your first priority is the kingdom of God, and you deeply believe that righteousness will satisfy. You have sought God's will for a certain direction, and you believe that He has led you to make specific plans. The problem is you are still worried about whether your plans will come about as you had hoped. How can you cast your anxiety upon Christ? For this exercise refer to the following Anxiety Worksheet.

First, state the problem. Remember, a problem well stated is half solved. In anxious states of mind, people can't see the forest for the trees. Put the problem in perspective. Will it matter for eternity? Generally speaking, the process of worrying takes a greater toll on a person than the negative consequences of what they worried about. Many anxious people only need to have their problems clarified.

The danger at this juncture is to seek ungodly counsel. The world is glutted with magicians and sorcerers who will promise incredible results. Their appearance may be striking. Their credentials may be impressive. Their personality may be charming but their character bankrupt. Jesus warned that we should judge righteously not according to appearance (see John 7:24). "How blessed is the man who does not walk in the counsel of the wicked, nor stand in the path of sinners, nor sit in the seat of scoffers!" (Psalm 1:1).

Second, divide the facts from the assumptions. We're anxious because we don't know what's going to happen tomorrow. Since we don't know, we make assumptions. A peculiar trait of the mind is its tendency to assume the worst. If the assumption is accepted as truth, it will drive the mind into its anxiety limits. If you act upon the assumption, you will be counted amongst the fools! Therefore, as best as possible, verify all the assumptions.

Third, determine what you have the right or ability to control. You are responsible only for those things that you have the right and ability to control. You are not responsible for those that you don't. Your success and sense of worth is tied only to that for which you are responsible. If you aren't living a responsible life, you should feel anxious! Don't try to cast your responsibility onto Christ; He will throw it back. But do cast your anxiety onto Him, because His integrity is at stake in meeting your needs if you are living a responsible life.

Fourth, list everything that you can do which is related to the situation that is under your responsibility. When people don't assume their responsibility, they turn to temporary cures for their anxiety. "The work of righteousness will be peace" (Isaiah 32:17). Turning to an unrighteous solution will only increase the anxiety in the future.

Fifth, once you are sure that you have fulfilled your responsibility, then see if there is any way you can help others. Finally, all the rest is God's responsibility, except for your responsibility to pray according to Philippians 4:6-8:

> Be anxious for nothing, but in everything by prayer and supplication with thanksgiving let your requests be made known to God. And the peace of God, which surpasses all comprehension, shall guard your hearts and your minds in Christ Jesus. Finally, brethren, whatever is true, whatever is honorable, whatever is right, whatever is pure, whatever is lovely, whatever is of good repute, if there is any excellence and if anything worthy of praise, let your mind dwell on these things.

Any residual sense of anxiety is probably due to assuming responsibilities that God never intended for you to have.

Anxiety Worksheet

1. State the problem.

2. Divide the facts from the assumptions:

    a. Facts relating to the situation

    b. Assumptions relating to the situation

    c. Verify the above assumptions

3. Determine what you have the right or ability to control.

    a. What you can control as a matter of personal responsibility

    b. What you have no right or ability to control

4. List everything related to the situation that is your responsibility.

5. If you have fulfilled your responsibility, how can you help others?

6. The rest is God's responsibility except for your responsibility to pray according to Philippians 4:6:

> "Be anxious for nothing, but in everything by prayer and supplication with thanksgiving let your requests be made known to God."

G. Personalizing the Truth ....

Internalize the truth by personalizing the Scripture and confessing it. Psalm 121 is personalized as an example:

> Where do I look for help? I look to the Creator of the universe. He cares so much about me that He watches over every step I take. He never gets tired or needs to sleep, so He's always watching over me. I can look to Him for whatever I need. He watches over me night and day and there are no unexpected surprises to fear. He does it every day and will do it forever.

Personalize any other Scriptures that God has revealed to you.

Get into the habit of renouncing the lies you have believed and announcing the truth out loud and often. (If you can't do it out loud, do it in your mind.)

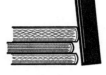

Reading Assignment: Chapter 10 in *Freedom from Addiction*

Freedom from the Past and Victory over Sin

The Overcomer's Covenant in Christ

Statement Seven

I renounce every unrighteous use of my body and I commit myself to no longer be conformed to this world, but rather to be transformed by the renewing of my mind. I choose to believe the truth and walk in it regardless of my feelings or circumstances. I know that before I came to Christ my mind was programmed according to this world and I used my body as an instrument of unrighteousness, thereby allowing sin to reign in my mortal body (see Romans 6:12,13).

The two most critical and basic issues that confront every born-again Christian may be summarized as follows: Do something about the neutral disposition of your physical body and be transformed by the renewing of your mind. Paul wrote, "I urge you therefore, brethren, by the mercies of God, to present your bodies a living and holy sacrifice, acceptable to God, which is your spiritual service of worship. And do not be conformed to this world, but be transformed by the renewing of your mind, that you may prove what the will of God is, that which is good and acceptable and perfect" (Romans 12:1,2).

Scripture assures us that we are alive in Christ and dead to sin because of the great work of Christ on the cross and in His resurrection (see Romans 6:1-11). We cannot do for ourselves what Christ has already done for us, but Romans 6:12 teaches that it is our responsibility to not allow sin to reign in our mortal bodies, obeying its lusts. The next verse tells us how. "And do not go on presenting the members of your body to sin as instruments of unrighteousness; but present yourselves to God as those alive from the dead, and your members as instruments of righteousness to God" (Romans 6:13).

Every time we commit a sexual sin or abuse our bodies with an excessive use of any substance, we are using our bodies as instruments of unrighteousness. We are allowing sin to reign in our mortal bodies. James 4:1 says, "What is the source of quarrels and conflicts among you? Is not the source your pleasures that wage war in your members?" Complete repentance would require us to renounce every use of our bodies as instruments of unrighteousness, present our bodies to God as living sacrifices and then be transformed by the renewing of our minds.

"Do you not know that your body is a temple of the Holy Spirit who is in you, whom you have from God, and that you are not your own? For you have been bought with a price: therefore glorify God in your body" (1 Corinthians 6:19,20). We are violating the temple of God with substance abuse or sexual sins. In doing so we have allowed sin to reign in our mortal bodies. We have become enslaved to the lusts of our flesh instead of disciplining our bodies and making them our slaves (see 1 Corinthians 9:27). Scripture exhorts us to be filled and controlled by the Holy Spirit rather than filling our lives and bodies with things that destroy us.

We were all born into this world physically alive, but spiritually dead (see Ephesians 2:1). During the formative years of our lives, we had neither the presence of God nor the knowledge of His ways. We all learned to live our lives independent from God. Some of us turned to alcohol, sex, drugs, food or other distractions as a means of coping, escaping the pressures of life or seeking pleasure. When we were born again, we became new creations in Christ, but everything that was programmed into our minds was still there. We must be transformed by the renewing of our minds. It will never be enough to try to change our behavior; we must change what we believe. People don't always live what they profess, but they will always live what they believe.

A. Understanding the Problem

Not knowing who they were in Christ is the one common denominator of every defeated Christian with whom we have worked. The fact that they all felt guilty is the second most common symptom of defeat. Paralyzed by guilt and having no sense of who they are in Christ, they conclude that they are nothing more than a product of their past. Many believe their sins are forgiven and they are going to heaven, but they don't understand their position in Christ which frees them from who they were in Adam. Consequently, they live mentally and emotionally in bondage to past failures and bad relationships. They know they're going to heaven, but in the meantime, it's a "mean" time. Christ didn't just come to pay the fare and punch our tickets for the heaven-bound train. He came to give us a new life, free us from the past and give us victory over the penalty *and* the power of sin.

B. Making a Personal Appraisal

If there is no condemnation for those who are in Christ Jesus (see Romans 8:1), why do you still feel guilty?

How has the sense of guilt and shame affected the way you perceived yourself, the way you live now and have lived in the past?

What effect would it have on your life (or the life of anyone struggling with addictive behaviors) if you knew you were totally forgiven and sensed it in your inner person?

What are the primary relationships and experiences in your life that you believe have made you the person you are today? Consider your parents, siblings and relatives, good and bad relationships, school and work experiences, successes, failures, disappointments with people, good and bad circumstances, etc., and list them here:

Do you believe that life in general has been unfair to you? Why?

Generally speaking, whom do you have a tendency to blame for your present condition (i.e. God, Satan, yourself, others, life itself)?

What good does blaming anything or anyone do? Will it resolve anything?

Do you believe that God has and is presently giving you a chance to start over again? Why or why not?

Since we are all born physically alive but spiritually dead in a fallen world and we live with fallen people who have a profound effect on our lives, what do you believe God has done in the past and will do presently to set you free from the outside influences of your past, present and future?

Why do you need God?

God has already done everything He needs to do for you to live a free and productive life in Christ. God has paid the penalty for all your sins—past, present and future. He has made you a new creation in Christ and He has defeated the devil. You are now seated with Him in the heavenlies so you have the authority to do God's will. He has given you the Holy Spirit who will guide you into all truth. That truth will set you free in Christ.

> **The Lie:**
> I am nothing more than a product of my past. I am a hopeless, helpless victim of a sick world and am guilty of many sins that I am unable to overcome.

C. Discovering the Truth That Will Set You Free

Remember that the key to freedom is knowing the truth. Pray the following prayer adapted from Ephesians 1:17-19 before you begin this section of discovering the truth that sets you free.

Dear Heavenly Father,
I am asking again that You would give me the Spirit of wisdom and revelation, so that I may know You better. I pray also that the eyes of my heart may be enlightened in order that I may know the hope to which You have called me, the riches of Your glorious inheritance in the saints and Your incomparably great power for us who believe. In Jesus' name, I pray. Amen.

Before answering the following questions, reread pages 243-252 in Chapter 10 of *Freedom from Addiction*.
Read Romans 6:1-4.

What does Paul say is the reason that you *can* stop sinning?

What did God do for you in order to make this possible?

What was the purpose of God doing this for you? In other words, what benefit do you get from it?

Read Romans 6:5-7.
You are united with Christ in His death, but also in His _____.

What is the truth you need to know to no longer be a slave to sin?

Who died with Christ?

Who has been freed from sin?

How are you freed from sin?

Read Romans 6:8-10.

For what purpose did you (the old person that you were before you became a Christian) die with Christ?

Since Christ has died and you died with Him and Christ was raised up from the dead and you were raised up with Him, what power does sin have over you?

What does God say is the purpose for your life now?

Read Romans 8:1,2.

When you have blatantly sinned—blown it bad and really messed up—how much condemnation will you get from God?

Is the law of sin and death still a factor to be dealt with in your life? Why or why not?

How did Jesus overcome the law of sin and death in your life?

Explain why being alive *in* Christ and identified with Him in His death, burial, resurrection and ascension are the only bases for being able to overcome the power of sin and death.

Why must your faith be based in the Word of God rather than what you feel or what others say?

What is the Galatians' heresy and how does it relate to you and your struggle with addictive behavior (see Galatians 3:1-5)?

Explain why it is so important to realize that it is not what you do that determines who you are, but who you are that determines what you do.

Read Romans 6:8-13.

In light of what God has done for you and since He has included you in His victory over sin and death, what is your first responsibility (see v. 11)?

Is this responsibility something you must do, or is it something you must believe?

If you really believed the truth that you are dead to sin, how do you think it would affect your life?

What are the two things God tells us not to do (see vv. 12,13)?

What do you need to believe and count on to be able to not do those two things (see vv. 8,11)?

What two positive actions are you to take (v. 13)?

Why is sin no longer your master (v. 14)?

How would living under law be different than living in God's grace?

Since you are no longer under the law, why shouldn't you go on sinning so that God's grace may abound?

Why is grace not a license to sin?

Reread Romans 6:1-14 and list the things that God has done on your behalf to make you a new person in Christ and free from sin and death.

1.

2.

3.

4.

5.

6.

7.

8.

9.

10.

Write a short paragraph summarizing how living by faith in Christ, based on what He has done for you, can set you free from the power of sin and death.

 .... # D. Stating the Truth

The truth that sets you free is based on what God has done on your behalf through Jesus Christ's death, burial and resurrection. What is true about Jesus is true about you because you are *in* Him. Remember, the two biggest mistakes Christians commonly make is trying to become someone they already are and trying to get something they already have. Victory is assured when we walk by faith based on who we are in Christ and what we already have because we are in Christ.

> The Truth:
> Since I am alive in Christ, I am no longer just a product of my past. I am a new creation in Christ and identified with Him in His death, burial, resurrection and ascension and I am seated with Him in the heavenlies. The law of life in Christ Jesus has set me free from the law of sin and death. I am free from sin and it is no longer my master because I am not under the law, but I am under grace and alive in Christ who has conquered sin and death.

Record any other truths you have learned.

E. Illustrating the Truth ·············

Read pages 130 and 131 in *Freedom from Addiction*, beginning with the section, "Praise the Lord, I'm dead!" and ending with "...freedom Christ purchased for us." How does this relate to you?

F. Appropriating the Truth ·············

From your personal study and group interaction, add to the following table:

The Lie That Binds You	The Truth That Sets You Free
I renounce the lie that: *Because of what I've done and what was done to me, I'm an addict.*	I announce the truth that: *Because of what Christ has done, I'm free from my past and sin.*

G. Personalizing the Truth

Internalize the truth by personalizing Scripture and confessing it. The following passage is taken from *The Message,* a paraphrase of the New Testament by Eugene Peterson:

So what do we do? Keep on sinning so God can keep on forgiving? I should hope not! If we've left the country where sin is sovereign, how can we still live in our old house there? Or didn't you realize we packed up and left there for good? This is what happened in baptism. When we went under the water, we left the old country of sin behind; when we came up out of the water, we entered into the new country of grace—a new life in a new land!

That's what baptism into the life of Jesus means. When we are lowered into the water, it is like the burial of Jesus; when we are raised up out of the water, it is like the resurrection of Jesus. Each of us is raised into a light-filled world by our Father so that we can see where we're going in our new grace-sovereign country.

Could it be any clearer? Our old way of life was nailed to the Cross with Christ, a decisive end to that sin-miserable life—no longer at sin's every beck and call! What we believe is this: If we get included in Christ's sin-conquering death, we also get included in his life-saving resurrection. We know that when Jesus was raised from the dead it was a signal of the end of death was the end of death-as-the-end. Never again will death have the last word. When Jesus died, he took sin down with him, but alive he brings God down to us. From now on, think of it this way: Sin speaks a dead language that means nothing to you; God speaks your mother tongue, and you hang on every word. You are dead to sin and alive to God. That's what Jesus did.

That means you must not give sin a vote in the way you conduct your lives. Don't give it the time of day. Don't even run little errands that are connected with that old way of life. Throw yourself wholeheartedly and full-time—remember , you've been raised from the dead!—into God's way of doing things. Sin can't tell you how to live. After all, you're not living under that old tyranny any longer. You're living in the freedom of God (Romans 6:1-14).

Personalize other Scripture passages that God has revealed to you concerning your life in Christ and freedom from sin.

Are you in the habit of renouncing the lies you have believed and announcing the truth out loud and often? (If you can't do it out loud, do it in your mind.)

Reading Assignment: Chapters 7 and 11 in *Freedom from Addiction*

Freedom from Performance-Based Acceptance

....

The Overcomer's Covenant in Christ

Statement Eight

I commit myself to take every thought captive to the obedience of Christ, and choose to think upon that which is true, honorable, right, pure and lovely. I know that the Holy Spirit explicitly says that in later times some will fall away from the faith, paying attention to deceitful spirits and doctrines, or teachings of demons (see 1 Timothy 4:1).

In the High Priestly Prayer, Jesus prays, "'I do not ask Thee to take them out of the world, but to keep them from the evil one. They are not of the world, even as I am not of the world. Sanctify them in the truth; Thy word is truth'" (John 17:15-17). Paul wrote, "I am afraid, lest as the serpent deceived Eve by his craftiness, your minds should be led astray from the simplicity and purity of devotion to Christ" (2 Corinthians 11:3). There is a battle going on for the minds of all believers; hence the necessity to take every thought captive to the obedience of Christ (see 2 Corinthians 10:5).

When we put on the armor of God, we take up the shield of faith which enables us to extinguish the flaming missiles of the evil one (see Ephesians 6:16). The way we overcome the father of lies (see John 8:44) is by choosing the truth of God's Word. Jesus said, "'If you abide in My word, then you are truly disciples of Mine; and you shall know the truth, and the truth shall make you free'" (John 8:31,32). We are not called to dispel the darkness. We are called to turn on the light. We do this by choosing to believe the truth of God's Word.

> Finally, brethren, whatever is true, whatever is honorable, whatever is right, whatever is pure, whatever is lovely, whatever is of good repute, if there is any excellence and if anything worthy of praise, let your mind dwell on these things. The things you have learned and received and heard and seen in me, practice these things; and the God of peace shall be with you (Philippians 4:8,9).

A. Understanding the Problem ··········

The shelves of Christian bookstores are lined with books telling us how to live the Christian life. There are how-to books on reading your Bible, prayer, fasting, witnessing, parenting, being a good wife or husband, ad infinitum. Have we fallen into the error of the Galatian church, believing that we were saved by faith, but we are now being perfected by the works of the law? If we performed better, would God love us more? If we just tried harder, would we finally overcome our addictive behaviors, or would we drive ourselves into burnout and defeat?

Nobody is more driven than those who struggle with addictive behaviors. Their hope is to find the ultimate how-to strategy, program or technique that will enable them to overcome their addiction by themselves without anybody ever knowing about their problem in the first place. But our hope is in Jesus Christ. He is our life and He is our victory. Recovery ministries ask us to obey certain laws, or principles. But Jesus calls us to respond by faith according to what God says is true. Then we will be able to walk by the power of the Holy Spirit rather than be enslaved to our fleshly desires.

········· B. Making a Personal Appraisal

Complete the following personal appraisal by evaluating yourself on a scale of 1 being the lowest to 5 being the highest, and then complete each statement:

Personal Appraisal

	Low				High
1. How successful are you?	1	2	3	4	5

I would be more successful if…

2. How significant are you?	1	2	3	4	5

I would be more significant if…

3. How fulfilled are you?	1	2	3	4	5

I would be more fulfilled if…

4. How satisfied are you?	1	2	3	4	5

I would be more satisfied if…

5. How happy are you?	1	2	3	4	5

I would be happier if…

	Low				High
6. How much fun are you having?	1	2	3	4	5

I would have more fun if...

7. How secure are you?	1	2	3	4	5

I would be more secure if...

8. How peaceful are you?	1	2	3	4	5

I would have more peace if...

What has been your greatest failure(s) in life?

What caused the failure(s)?

How are you trying to get over the failure(s)?

Why do you think it was a failure?

Are you a failure? A mistake is never a failure unless you fail to learn from it. To stumble and fall is not failure. To stumble and fall again is still not failure. Failure is when you say you were pushed. Were you pushed? Have you failed to learn by your mistakes?

What the devil meant for evil, God intends for good. How can your past mistakes be stepping stones to a successful life?

Think of another person who has a great testimony of being delivered from bondage to freedom like Mike and Julia have been. How is God using that person in a powerful way?

Can that happen to you? Why or why not?

How did your parents judge success as it related to them and to you as their child?

Summarize your philosophy of life as it relates to success.

How is it the same or different from your parents' philosophy?

How is it different from God's definition of success?

Are you a perfectionist? If so, why?

Are you a driven person? If so, why?

Who are you trying to impress, be accepted by or gain the approval of? Why?

Do you accept yourself just the way you are? The question is not, Are you totally satisfied with your ability to perform? but Do you accept yourself as a lovable worthwhile person?

What would you have to do or accomplish in order to fully accept yourself?

Does God accept you just the way you are?

Have your parents accepted you the way you are or do you feel as though you never quite measured up to their expectations?

Were you, or are you still, driven to earn their approval?

What if they will never approve of you and what you have done with your life?

Read Romans 3:21-26 and 4:7,8.

If you can't accept yourself the way you are, you need to change the basis for self-acceptance to be the same as God's. On what basis does God accept you?

> **The Lie:**
> I cannot accept myself nor can God or others accept me unless I live a perfect life. If I try harder and perform better, God and others will accept me and then I can accept myself.

C. Discovering the Truth That Sets You Free

Remember that the key to freedom is knowing the truth. Pray the following prayer adapted from Ephesians 1:17-19 before you begin this section of discovering the truth that sets you free.

> Dear Heavenly Father,
> I ask that You would once again give me the Spirit of wisdom and revelation, so that I may know You better. I pray also that the eyes of my heart may be enlightened in order that I may know the hope to which You have called me, the riches of Your glorious inheritance in the saints and Your incomparably great power for us who believe. In Jesus' name, I pray. Amen.

Referring back to the Personal Appraisal chart on pages 155-156, how did you complete the "I would be more...if..." statements? If your answers were dependent upon the approval or acceptance of others and favorable circumstances, you are setting yourself up for a fall.

Success is related to goals, but who is determining the goals for your life? What may be a legitimate goal for one person is impossible for another. Understand that you can be successful in the eyes of the world and a complete failure in the eyes of God. Success is accepting God's goal for your life and becoming what He has called you to be by His grace.

Read Joshua 1:7-9; and 3 John 2 and explain how you could live a successful life by faith.

Significance is related to time. What is forgotten in time is of little significance, what is remembered for eternity is of greatest significance. Read Acts 5:33-40; 1 Corinthians 3:13,14 and 1 Timothy 4:7,8. Explain how you could live a significant life by faith.

Fulfillment is related to our role fulfillment or our calling in life. Not everybody has the same role to fulfill. Fulfillment comes when we discover our own uniqueness in Christ and use our gifts to edify others and glorify the Lord. Read Matthew 25:14-30; 2 Timothy 4:5 and Romans 12:1-8. Describe how you could live a fulfilling life by faith.

Satisfaction is related to quality, not quantity. We will never be satisfied by doing a lot of things in a mediocre way. Satisfaction is living righteously and seeking to raise the quality of relationships, service and products. Read Matthew 5:6 and 2 Timothy 4:7. Explain how you can live a satisfied life by faith.

True happiness is being content with what we have. All advertising is an attempt to get us to believe that if we only buy their product we would be happy. The real problem is we don't focus on what we already have. We have the presence of God in our lives and He will meet all our needs. Our sins have been forgiven and we will live together with God for all eternity. Happiness is being thankful for what He has already given you because happy are the people who are content with what they have! Read Philippians 4:12; 1 Thessalonians 5:16-18 and 1 Timothy 6:6-8. How can you have a happy and thankful life?

Fun is uninhibited spontaneity. The secret is to remove nonscriptural inhibitors, like "What will people say?" We are no longer chained to our past or to the traditions of mankind. We are liberated in Christ. We don't have to drink or use drugs to free ourselves from our inhibitions. There is joy in the presence of God. Read 2 Samuel 6:20-23; Romans 14:22 and Galatians 1:10; 5:1. Explain how you could have a lot more fun living the Christian life if you walked by faith.

Security is related to our eternal relationship with God. Insecurity is depending upon temporal things that we have no right or ability to control. Read John 10:27-30; Romans 8:31-39 and Ephesians 1:13,14. How can you have a greater sense of security when you walk by faith?

Peace is related to the internal order of our lives not the external order. Notice the prepositions in the following:

Peace *with* God:	This we have!
Peace *of* God:	This we need!
Peace *on* earth:	This we want!

Read Isaiah 32:17; Jeremiah 6:14; John 14:27 and Philippians 4:6,7. Discover how you can have a greater sense of peace if you walk by faith.

Paul wrote his letter to the Galatians because some false teachers had came to Galatia after Paul had left. They were teaching that the law must be observed to be saved and live a good Christian life. Paul had some very strong words for such false teachers. He warned them that they were deserting Christ and turning to a different gospel (see Galatians 1:6); that the gospel was being perverted (see Galatians 1:7); and that they should be eternally condemned for teaching false doctrine.

Why did Paul have such strong words for those who were teaching the law rather than the gospel of grace?

Read Romans 7:4-7.

Why does your relationship with the law have to be ended?

What problems does living by the law cause for you?

What is the better way that Christ has introduced for us to live and serve Him?

Read Galatians 2:4,5. What does legalistic teaching threaten?

Read Galatians 2:19-21.

What is the believer's relation to the law?

What is our new identity and how should we live now?

If righteousness (living a right life) could be gained by observing the law, what would be unnecessary?

Read Galatians 3:1-14.

How did we receive the Spirit (see v. 2)?

How will God work miracles and accomplish His will in your life (see v. 5)?

How did Abraham obtain righteousness (see vv. 6-9)?

What will happen if you try to live victoriously by observing the law?

How should we live the Christian life (see v. 11)?

What did Christ's death on the cross accomplish for us (see vv. 13-15)?

Read Galatians 3:23-29.

What was the purpose of the law?

What is your relation to the law now?

What is your identity as a Christian now?

Read Galatians 4:1-11.

Why did Christ redeem us from the law?

Since we have been redeemed from the law, what is our position as Christians now?

In what way are you tempted to turn back to weak and miserable principles and what would be the result if you did?

Read Galatians 5:1-6.

What is your responsibility?

How has your life been burdened by legalism (i.e. trying to earn God's approval by living under the law)?

If we let ourselves do this, what are the results (see verse 4)?

What will be the evidence in your life that you are not under law?

Note: The grace of God is not a license to sin. We have been called to live a righteous life, but we cannot keep the law in our own strength. The law is not sinful, but legalism is. In a broader sense, the law of God reflects the moral principles that govern the universe. Yet we cannot have a righteous relationship with God by observing the law. The law leads us to Christ. He has met the just demands of the law for us. We can now live a righteous life, but only if we walk by faith in the power of the Holy Spirit.

D. Stating the Truth

> **The Truth:**
> I am no longer under the curse of the law. Christ became
> a curse for me by satisfying the just demands of the law. I
> now live by faith in the power of the Holy Spirit. I can be
> holy as He is holy only by the grace of God.

Record any other truths that you have learned.

E. Illustrating the Truth

Read the section entitled "The Stronghold of Self-Help on pages 176-
182 in *Freedom from Addiction*." How do these pages relate to you?

F. Appropriating the Truth

The Lie That Binds You	The Truth That Sets You Free
I renounce the lie that:	I announce the truth that:
I need to make myself worthy. *I need to merit God's acceptance.* *I will achieve righteousness.*	*I have been made worthy.* *He has given me His acceptance.* *I will receive righteousness.*

Add to the list those lies that you have believed and the truth that you have now learned.

G. Personalizing the Truth

Internalize the truth by personalizing the Scripture and confessing what you have learned in your private study as well as what you have learned from your group.

> For example:
> Because of the death of Christ on the cross and His resurrection, I do not have to earn God's approval. I am alive in Christ and dead to sin (see Romans 6:1-7).

Personalize any Scripture passages that have been meaningful to you.

> For example:
> I am no longer condemned because I am in Christ Jesus. The law of life in Christ Jesus has set me free from the law of sin and death (Romans 8:1,2).

Have you fully established the habit of renouncing the lies you have believed and announcing the truth out loud and often? (If you can't do it out loud, do it in your mind.)

The Battle for the Mind

Reading Assignment: Chapter 12 in *Freedom from Addiction*

....

The Overcomer's Covenant in Christ

--- **Statement Nine** ---

I commit myself to God's great goal for my life to conform to His image. I know that I will face many trials, but God has given me the victory and I am not a victim, but an overcomer in Christ. The grace of God will enable me to triumph over every trial resulting in proven character.

Salvation ensures us that we are forgiven and alive in Christ, but God isn't finished with us yet. We have "laid aside the old self with its evil practices, and have put on the new self who is being renewed to a true knowledge according to the image of the One who created him" (Colossians 3:9,10). God's will for our lives is our sanctification (see 1 Thessalonians 4:3). Sanctification conforms us to His image as we grow in Christlike character. Bondage to alcohol, sex, drugs, etc. has arrested our growth in character. When life became difficult, we chose the path of sin that seemed easier or more fun rather than the path of sanctification.

Paul taught the right path of hope. "We...exult in our tribulations, knowing that tribulation brings about perseverance; and perseverance, proven character; and proven character, hope; and hope does not disappoint, because the love of God has been poured out within our hearts through the Holy Spirit who was given to us" (Romans 5:3-5). Drowning our sorrows or running away from our problems does not resolve them or cause them to go away. It only makes them worse. Our hope lies in the proven character that comes by facing the hard issues of life and deciding to hang in there and grow up. This is God's goal for our lives and it's made possible by the Holy Spirit who indwells us.

A. Understanding the Problem ··········

When I (Mike) teach at a Christian treatment center, I always tell the group, "If you have a problem, don't focus on your behavior, look at the belief that causes the behavior. What you are believing (or disbelieving) determines what you do. 'For as he thinks within himself, so he is'" (Proverbs 23:7). Nobody can do anything without first thinking it. If we want to change our behavior, we must change the way we think and consequently what we believe. It won't do you any good to work this program (or any program) if you do not change what you believe and how you think.

Repentance means a change of mind. King David gives us an example of his repentance from his sin with Bathsheba when he wrote in Psalm 51:6 "Behold, Thou dost desire truth in the innermost being, and in the hidden part Thou wilt make me know wisdom." Many people will enter treatment programs, submit to their strict discipline and with the support of the group change their behavior for a period of time. But unless they change what they believe, when the external support is removed, most will probably fall back into the addictive behaviors within weeks or months after they leave. When the program doesn't bring the desired results, they feel even greater condemnation and even more like a failure. Changing behavior will not by itself change the person. If it did, the law would be sufficient to set us free. The following testimony given to Neil illustrates this in a powerful way:

> The fact that I was born again couldn't be seen by those who had the opportunity to observe my life. I still held on to the lie that I was a no-good, drunken, sex-crazed man that would only be locked away for the rest of my life. My mind was full of all sorts of wicked and vile imaginations. I was a very passive individual concerning spiritual things. When a thought came to my mind, I accepted it as my own and acted it out. My Christian friends would see me speaking of the Lord in a partially sound mind, and then I would be drunk and cursing people with all kinds of wicked words and

actions. I have been arrested and my godly wife divorced me as I was an unfaithful husband. My spiritual life was in shambles.

I went to my church for one last bit of hope. My pastor was strong in his words which caused me to search my heart. He recommended two of your books, *Victory over the Darkness*, and *The Bondage Breaker*. The light seemed to go off inside my spirit to the truth of the gospel. I began to see my worth in Christ and that I am a child of God. My earthly father had rejected me from birth, and I was molested as a child. Having no truth foundation, I was in bondage to my past. I would even hurt myself and then ask God if that pleased Him. The evil one made me think of God in a sick and perverted way.

Now I have learned to take every thought captive in obedience to Christ. Since I have learned to judge every thought by the word of God my life has dramatically changed. I no longer see myself as a worthless worm that could never do even the simplest of tasks. I am able to see myself as a new creation in Christ. My mind is a lot clearer now, and I am able to love my Heavenly Father and receive His love. My friends who had all given up on me and turned me over to the Lord in frustration tell me they have seen such a change in my behavior. It is true that if a person sees who they are in Christ, they will act accordingly.

B. Making a Personal Appraisal

What have you been told or believed is wrong with you?

What have you been told or believed that you must start doing or stop doing in order to change what is wrong with you?

How has that worked for you?

In recovery ministries and treatment centers they talk about "stinking thinking" and advise you not to listen to the "committee in your head." What has been the nature of your "stinking thinking," (i.e. what kind of thoughts have you struggled with about yourself, God and what you must or must not do)?

How has your thought life affected your perception of God, yourself and contributed to your struggle with addictive behaviors?

Have you experienced the peace of God which surpasses all comprehension, that will guard your heart and mind in Christ Jesus (see Philippians 4:7)? When and how did you come to experience that peace?

The problem is not what you have done or are still doing. The real issue is who you are and what you believe. Our minds have been programmed externally by the world we were raised in, our own flesh and the devil. We now have the mind of Christ because we are partakers of the divine nature, and the Holy Spirit will lead us into all truth. We have to learn to take every thought captive to the obedience of Christ and renew our minds to the truth of God's Word.

> ### The Lie:
> **If I submit to a program and change my behavior I will free myself from my addiction.**

C. Discovering the Truth That Sets You Free

Remember that the key to freedom is knowing the truth. Pray the following prayer adapted from Ephesians 1:17-19 before you begin this section of discovering the truth that sets you free.

> Dear Heavenly Father,
> I again ask that You would give me the Spirit of wisdom and revelation so that I may know You better. I pray also that the eyes of my heart may be enlightened in order that I may know the hope to which You have called me, the riches of Your glorious inheritance in the saints and Your incomparably great power for us who believe. In Jesus' name, I pray. Amen.

Read John 8:31-36.

What does Jesus say is the requirement to be free?

If truth sets you free, what will keep you in bondage?

What is the evidence that a person is not free?

Jesus says that being a part of His family is essential for freedom. Are you a slave or a son? In what ways do you act more like a slave than a son?

Since sons are free, is it possible that you have believed the lie that you are a slave to sin and therefore in bondage to it? Explain.

How complete is the freedom that Jesus promised?

Do you believe that freedom is possible for you? Why or why not?

Read 2 Corinthians 10:3-5.

How have your thoughts been raised up against the knowledge of God?

What does it mean to take "every thought captive to the obedience of Christ"? How can you do that?

Note: What must be destroyed are the fortresses in your mind. The *King James Version* and the *New International Version* of the Bible use the word "strongholds." Strongholds are habit patterns of thought which are burned into our minds over time or through traumatic experiences. Ed Silvoso defines a "stronghold" as "a mindset impregnated with hopelessness which causes us to accept as unchangeable what is known to be contrary to the will of God." Every addiction is a mental stronghold. As long as we believe the lie that the situation is hopeless and that we are unchangeable, we will stay in bondage.

Why must the weapons of our warfare be divinely powerful?

Is the battle for our minds psychological, neurological or spiritual? What percentage would you assign to each part?

Regardless of where the thoughts come from, whose responsibility is it to win the battle for our minds?

We estimate that about 15 percent of the Bible-believing community are living free and productive lives in Christ. About 70 percent struggle with their thought lives, having little peace of mind. They find it difficult to concentrate when they read their Bibles and pray, and they have little if any understanding of who they are in Christ. Most of these people could process the Steps to Freedom in Christ on their own and gain a degree of freedom that they have never experienced before. The primary reason they haven't lived free and productive lives is they have never been established complete in Christ, and they have never understood the battle for their minds nor had an opportunity to comprehensively repent of their sins. The other 15 percent are in total bondage. They can't read their Bibles nor process the steps on their own. They fill institutions or wander the streets in a drunken stupor carrying on a conversation with someone nobody else can hear or see. Many drink to drown out the voices in their heads.

If the above figures are even close to the truth, how do you relate them to your struggle to get free in Christ?

In *The Message* Eugene Peterson paraphrases 2 Corinthians 10:5: "We use our powerful God-tools for smashing warped philosophies, tearing down barriers erected against the truth of God, fitting every loose thought and emotion and impulse into the structure of life shaped by Christ."

What are some of the loose or impulsive thoughts and emotions that you struggle with in your mind?

Read 1 Corinthians 14:20 and 1 Peter 1:13.

These two passages point out our responsibility to think maturely and prepare our minds for action. In what ways have you not assumed your responsibility to think as a mature adult and how could you change that?

The most spiritually dangerous thing we can do mentally is to passively entertain any thoughts that come to our minds. We should never direct our thoughts inwardly or passively. The Bible always instructs us to actively use our minds and direct our thoughts outwardly, upwardly and positively. This is especially true when facing certain conflicts in our lives.

What possible conflicts do you foresee in troubling circumstances, difficult relationships and unresolved problems for which, according to the Word of God, you need to prepare your mind in advance so that you can take action and face them with confidence? Also consider the immature or deceptive thoughts that you have been prone to think in the past concerning the situation, and list them below.

Possible conflicts	Immature thinking or deception	Mature thinking or the truth

Read 1 Timothy 4:1.

Is there evidence that the things Paul warned us about are happening now? Explain your answer.

How can you know if you are paying attention to deceiving spirits?

Read 2 Corinthians 11:3. What is Paul's concern and is his concern valid for you?

Read 1 John 2:12-14.

How does John describe a child in the faith (v. 12)?

If a child of the faith has overcome the penalty of sin, how can the power of sin be overcome?

Read Colossians 3:15,16.

How can the peace of Christ rule in our hearts?

How can we let the Word of Christ richly dwell within us?

Letting the Word of Christ richly dwell within you is more than just having head knowledge of the Word. Describe what that means to you.

Do you think it is possible to have a knowledge of what God says, but not allow it to penetrate your heart in such a way as to transform your character?

If that were the case, would you be experiencing freedom in Christ? Explain.

Read Romans 12:1,2.

Why is it necessary to submit our bodies to God as living sacrifices?

Why is it necessary to renew our minds?

Can anyone prove the will of God is good, acceptable and perfect for them without transforming their minds? Why or why not?

Does someone have to prove that the will of God is good for us before we allow our minds to be transformed (i.e. Why should I spend time renewing my mind according to the Word of God; what good would it do me)?

Read Colossians 3:1-4.
How can you discipline yourself to...

1. Seek the things above?

2. Set your mind on the things above?

What four truths about ourselves are revealed in this passage that will help us accomplish this seeking and setting our minds on the things above without becoming legalistic?

Read Romans 8:5,6.

What two choices do we have in directing our minds?

What will be the result of setting our minds on the flesh which have been programmed to live independent from God?

What will be the result if we set our minds on the Spirit?

How can we discipline ourselves to direct our minds toward the Spirit?

You are not called to dispel the darkness; you are called to simply turn on the light. If you started rebuking every negative thought that came to your mind, that is all you would do for the rest of your life. You overcome the lie by choosing the truth. It doesn't make any difference where the thought comes from, the answer is the same: Choose the truth.

How would you do this according to Philippians 4:6-8?

If you could put into practice and never violate Philippians 4:8, what difference do you think it would make in your life?

In your relationships?

In your behavior?

Note: Would it be worth the effort to discipline your mind and renew it by taking every thought captive in obedience to Christ? I (Mike) was sharing this truth over lunch with a young man when he leaned across the table and asked in shock, "Do you mean I have to take *every* thought captive?"

"Only if you want to be free" I answered.

My wife, Julia, put it into proper perspective when she said, "It sounds like a lot of trouble to monitor your thought life until you consider the alternative." The alternative can only lead to defeat and bondage. The Greek word for repentance—*metanoia*—literally means "to change your mind." Any person unwilling to discipline his or her mind to the truth of God's Word will not experience the abundant life that we have in Christ.

D. Stating the Truth

How long will it take to renew your mind? It will take the rest of your life! It took all of your natural life to learn how to live independent from God. We don't recommend making vows and promises, but we do think it should be every Christian's goal to renew his or her mind to the truth recorded in God's Word and learn the discipline of taking every thought captive to the obedience of Christ.

> The Truth:
> I will be transformed when I renew my mind according to the truth of God's Word, and I will walk in freedom if I discipline my mind to take every thought captive in obedience to Christ.

Record any other truths that you have learned in your personal study or group discussion.

E. Illustrating the Truth ·········

Read the section entitled: "Clean Up Your Mind" on pages 295-296 in *Freedom from Addiction*. How does this illustration relate to you?

F. Appropriating the Truth ··········

The Lie That Binds You	The Truth That Sets You Free
I renounce the lie that:	I announce the truth that:
If I change my behavior, I'll change who I am as a person.	*If I believe the truth of who I am in Christ, my behavior will change.*
I am the problem. I need to change who I am..	*I have a problem. I need to know the truth to be free.*
The answer is: I must find the right program and work it.	*The answer is believing what God has done.*
It is too much trouble to discipline my mind.	*I get in too much trouble if I don't discipline my mind.*
The battle is external.	*The battle is in the mind.*

List other lies that you have believed and the truth that you have learned.

Failures come from "cannots," and success comes from "cans." Read through the following "Twenty Cans of Success":

Twenty Cans of Success[1]

1. Why should I say, "I can't" when the Bible says, "I can do all things through [Christ] who strengthens me" (Philippians 4:13)?

2. Why should my needs not be met knowing that "my God shall supply all [my] needs according to His riches in glory in Christ Jesus" (Philippians 4:19)?

3. Why should I fear when the Bible says that "God has not given [me] a spirit of fear, but of power and of love and of a sound mind" (2 Timothy 1:7, *NKJV*)?

4. Why should I doubt or lack faith knowing that "God has allotted to each a measure of faith" (Romans 12:3)?

5. Why am I weak when the Bible says, "the LORD is the strength of my life" (Psalm 27:1, *KJV*) and "people who know their God will display strength" (Daniel 11:32).

6. Why should I allow Satan to have supremacy over my life, for "greater is He who is in [me] than he who is in the world" (1 John 4:4)?

7. Why should I accept defeat when the Bible says, "thanks be to God, who always leads us in His triumph in Christ" (2 Corinthians 2:14)?

8. Why should I lack wisdom when Christ "became to us wisdom from God" (1 Corinthians 1:30) and God gives wisdom to all men generously and without reproach who ask Him for it (see James 1:5)?

9. Why should I be depressed when I can recall to my mind and therefore have hope that "the LORD's lovingkindnesses indeed never cease, for His compassions never fail. They are new every morning; great is Thy faithfulness" (Lamentations 3:22,23)?

10. Why should I worry and fret when I can cast all my anxiety upon Christ, because He cares for me (see 1 Peter 5:7)?

11. Why should I ever be in bondage, for "where the Spirit of the Lord is, there is liberty" (2 Corinthians 3:17) and "it was for freedom that Christ set [me] free" (Galatians 5:1)?

12. Why should I feel condemned when the Bible says, "There is...no condemnation for those who are in Christ Jesus" (Romans 8:1)?

13. Why should I ever feel alone when Jesus said, "I am with you always, even to the end of the age" (Matthew 28:20) and "I will never desert you, nor will I ever forsake you" (Hebrews 13:5)?

14. Why should I feel accursed or the victim of bad luck when the Bible says that "Christ redeemed us from the curse of the law, being made a curse for us...that we might receive the promise of the Spirit through faith" (Galatians 3:13,14, *KJV*)?

15. Why should I be discontented when I, like Paul, can learn "to be content in whatever circumstances I am" (Philippians 4:11)?

16. Why should I feel worthless when God "made Him who knew no sin to be sin on our behalf, that we might become the righteousness of God in Him" (2 Corinthians 5:21)?

17. Why should I ever have a persecution complex, for "if God is for [me], who is against [me]" (Romans 8:31)?

18. Why should I be confused "for God is not the author of confusion, but of peace" (1 Corinthians 14:33, *KJV*) and "now we have received, not the spirit of the world, but the Spirit who is from God, that we might know the things freely given to us by God" (1 Corinthians 2:12)?

19. Why should I feel like a failure when "in all these things we overwhelmingly conquer through Him who loved us" (Romans 8:37)?

20. Why should I let the world bother me when Jesus said, "'In the world you have tribulation, but take courage; I have overcome the world'" (John 16:33)?

G. Personalizing the Truth

Internalize the truth by personalizing the Scripture and confessing it.

> For example:
> Because the old sin-loving sinner that I was died with Christ, I am a new creation in Christ. Because He is my very life, I can choose to think about things that are true, right and pure and not listen to Satan's lies (from Colossians 3:1-4).

Personalize any Scriptures that God has revealed to you.

> An example from Philippians 4:6-10:
> I am not going to be anxious about anything. Instead I am going to God with my requests with an attitude of thanksgiving. I believe that the peace of God which surpasses my ability to comprehend will guard my heart and my mind in Christ Jesus. From now on I am going to discipline my mind to dwell on whatever is true, whatever is honorable, whatever is right, whatever is pure, whatever is lovely, whatever is of good repute and anything that is excellent or worthy of

praise. All the things that I have learned and received and heard and seen in Scripture and from the example of the apostle Paul and other mature Christian leaders I will put into practice and the peace of God will be in me.

By now you should be in the habit of renouncing the lies you have believed and announcing the truth out loud and often.

Note:

1. Adapted from Neil T. Anderson, *Victory over the Darkness* (Ventura, Calif.: Regal Books, 1990), pp. 115-117.

Growing in Grace

The Overcomer's Covenant in Christ

Statement Ten

I choose to adopt the attitude of Christ which is to do nothing from selfishness or empty conceit, but with humility of mind I will regard others as more important than myself; and not merely look out for my own personal interests, but also the interests of others (see Philippians 2:3-5). I know that, "'It is more blessed to give than to receive'" (Acts 20:35).

Excessive use of alcohol and drugs, having sex for our own pleasure and other addictive behaviors are the ultimate acts of selfishness. We must assume responsibility for our own character and seek to meet the needs of those around us. We all need acceptance and affirmation, but don't wait until others extend it to you. Commit yourself to love others as Christ has demonstrated His love for you. "We know love by this, that He laid down His life for us; and we ought to lay down our lives for the brethren. But whoever has the world's goods, and beholds his brother in need and closes his heart against him, how does the love of God abide in him? Little children, let us not love with word or with tongue, but in deed and truth" (1 John 3:16-18).

It is one of life's great compensations that we cannot sincerely help another person without helping ourselves in the process. We get out of life what we put into it. If you want a friend, be a friend. If you want someone to love you, love someone. Don't give people what they deserve, give them what they need. Whatever life asks of you, give just a little bit more. You will not only be living a responsible life, you will also enjoy a greater degree of freedom.

"Be merciful, just as your Father is merciful. And do not judge and you will not be judged; and do not condemn, and you shall not be condemned; pardon, and you will be pardoned. Give, and it will be given to you; good measure, pressed down, shaken together, running over, they will pour into your lap. For by your standard of measure, it will be measured to you in return" (Luke 6:36-38).

A. Understanding the Problem

When the Pharisees asked Jesus what the greatest commandment was, He replied, "'You shall love the Lord your God with all your heart, and with all your soul, and with all your mind.' This is the great and foremost commandment. The second is like it. 'You shall love your neighbor as yourself'" (Matthew 22:37-39). The whole purpose of the Bible is to instruct us how to fall in love with God and reflect His love to each other.

Many who are caught in addictive behaviors are self-absorbed. Being self-conscious, self-consumed and self-indulgent leaves no time or energy to love others unless it will gain for them the acceptance and approval they so desperately need. By definition, love is not self-centered. Love focuses on the needs of others. Bondage drives you away from others into isolation and self-degradation. Freedom releases you to love others. "You, my brothers, were called to be free. But do not use your freedom to indulge the sinful nature, rather serve one another in love" (Galatians 5:13, *NIV*).

Paul said, "The goal of our instruction is love from a pure heart and a good conscience and a sincere faith" (1 Timothy 1:5). Hopefully this study has helped you gain a pure heart, a good conscience and a sincere faith. During my (Mike's) period of addiction, I often wondered *How do I get going and move on in the Christian life?* For me it began when I finally came to the end of myself, gave up all my formulas, understood who I was in Christ and began to trust Jesus to be my life. My friend Steve McVey said, "For many years, I tried to make Jesus Lord, then I understood I could trust Him to be my *life*." We don't just need the words that Jesus (or Paul or John or Mike or Neil) said. We need Jesus.

B. Making a Personal Appraisal ··········

At first glance, which appears to be the most important?

Taking a seminary class	or	going out to eat with your family?
Going to visitation evangelism	or	watching your child play in a Little League game?
Going to prayer meeting	or	taking a meal to a shut-in?
Going to church on Sunday night	or	visiting a sick relative?
Going to a Bible Study	or	helping a neighbor?
Going to choir practice	or	spending time with a neighbor whose spouse has left him or her?
Going to an early morning discipleship group	or	getting kids off to school when your spouse is sick?
Attending your recovery group	or	reading to your child?

It is critically important to serve the Body of Christ by being involved in your local church programs, but all of your involvements should result in loving God and showing His love to others. Which side of the above list are you most committed to and why?

Read James 1:21-25.

How should we respond to the Word of God?

What should be the result of looking intently into God's Word?

If you could live your life over, where would you spend your time? Number the following list in order of preference:

____ Business   ____ Exercise   ____ Friends   ____ Family

____ Ministry   ____ Reading   ____ Church   ____ Pleasure

____ Other _____

Why did you number the list the way you did? How is that different now than the way you have lived your life in the past?

Do you know someone who was actively involved in church, and then fell morally and stopped attending church? Now when they are encouraged to go back to church, pray and read their Bible, they say, "I tried that once and it didn't work." Why didn't it work?

Can someone be active in church and not grow spiritually? Why or why not?

How would you define spiritual growth?

What would a spiritually mature Christian look like?

> **The Lie:**
> I will grow spiritually if I attend Christian programs regularly and not miss any of their meetings.

Note: We deeply believe that every Christian should be involved in church, but we also believe that every Christian church should be helping their people be alive and free in Christ. Some churches aren't committed to that, and others measure their success by attendance. There is no substitute for being involved in the Body of Christ where we build up one another.

C. Discovering the Truth That Sets You Free

Remember that the key to freedom is knowing the truth. Pray the following prayer adapted from Ephesians 1:17-19 before you begin this section of discovering the truth that sets you free:

Dear Heavenly Father,
I am asking again that You would give me the Spirit of wisdom and revelation, so that I may know You better. I pray also that the eyes of my heart may be enlightened in order that I may know the hope to which You have called me, the riches of Your glorious inheritance in the saints and Your incomparably great power for us who believe. In Jesus' name, I pray. Amen.

Read Luke 10:25-37.

What was the lawyer's question?

How did Jesus answer him?

How did the lawyer try to justify himself?

Who is our neighbor according to Jesus?

Do you see any resemblance between the two religious people who passed by on the other side and organized religions. Why or why not?

What does a good neighbor do (vv. 36,37)?

Read 1 John 4:7-12,19.

On what basis do we have the capacity to love one another?

What is the evidence that we are born of God and know Him?

What makes God's *agape* love unique is that it is not dependent upon the object of love. God loves us because He *is* love. It is His nature to love us. If the love of God was on any other basis, it would be conditional love. Now that we have become partakers of His divine nature, we have the capacity to love one another in a way that we could not apart from Christ. That becomes the primary measure of our maturity in Christ. The more we become like Christ, the more we are able to love our heavenly Father and all His creation.

How is the uniqueness of God's love to be expressed according to Luke 6:27-38?

Read 1 Corinthians 13:1-8.

What four things are worthless without love?

List the character qualities of love:

1.

2.

3.

4.

5.

6.

7.

8.

9.

10.

11.

12.

13.

Read John 13:34,35. What is the greatest evidence of our faith?

Read the following verses and explain how we can love one another better.

Romans 12:9-13

Philippians 2:3-8

1 John 3:16-18

1 John 4:7-12

Read John 15:1-8. What is the one thing that Jesus tells us to do in order to bear fruit and prove we are His disciples?

Note: Jesus said He is glorified if we bear fruit so we wrongly conclude that we *have* to bear fruit. But we don't! When we abide in Christ, we *will* bear fruit. Bearing fruit is the evidence of abiding in Christ. Christian growth is first and foremost a work of God. No growth will take place unless we abide in Christ and walk by the Spirit.

Read Colossians 2:6-10.

Notice that we are first "rooted *in Christ*," then "built up *in Christ*" in order to "walk *in Christ*." Verse 10 says we are complete in Christ. The point is we are incomplete without Christ. Every aspect of our Christian growth is dependent upon our relationship with Christ. Contrast recovery in Christ to the secular world's approach to recovery (see v. 8).

Read Galatians 5:24.

What is your responsibility as a child of God?

There is no such thing as a flesh improvement program. There are no better or worse ways to live independent from God. What improvement have you seen in your old nature (your flesh) since you became a Christian?

Read Galatians 5:16-18.

How can we not carry out the desires of the flesh?

Why is the flesh or old nature in opposition to the Holy Spirit?

How do we live or walk by the Spirit?

Read Ephesians 5:18-21.

What are the three characteristics, or attitudes, of a Christian who is filled with the Spirit?

Read Titus 2:11,12.

How can we say no to ungodliness and worldly passions and live righteously?

Note: Grace is God's unmerited and undeserved favor given to His children. Grace is God working in our lives, doing what we cannot do and giving us what we cannot achieve. Mercy is *not* giving us what we deserve. Grace is giving us what we *don't* deserve. Only by the grace of God can we live the Christian life because He is our life and our strength.

Read Romans 5:17.

If grace is God doing for us what we cannot do and giving us what we cannot earn, what *has* God done for us and what *does* He give us?

After each of the following verses, write "God has given me _____" or "God has done _____ for me."

Psalm 103:12

Romans 2:6,7

Romans 5:1

Romans 5:10

Romans 8:1,2

1 Corinthians 2:12

1 Corinthians 2:16

1 Corinthians 15:57

Ephesians 1:3

Ephesians 1:4

Ephesians 1:7

Ephesians 1:8

Ephesians 1:13,14

Ephesians 2:5

Ephesians 2:6,7

Philippians 3:9

Colossians 1:13

Colossians 2:14

Titus 1:2

2 Peter 1:3

Read Luke 10:38-41.

What was distracting Martha?

Contrast the personalities of Martha and Mary. Which one are you most like?

Jesus said, "Martha, you are worried and bothered about so many things" (v. 41). What things are more important to you than your relationship with God?

What things are more important to you than your relationship with your family?

What is the one necessary thing and how can you make sure that nothing else becomes more important?

Read 1 John 1:5-10.

Walking in the light is not moral perfection. It is living in constant agreement with God. Confession is agreeing with God and that is essentially the same as walking in the light. If we live by the truth, we will be walking in the light. What are the two results of walking in the light?

Denial is probably the greatest obstacle for those struggling with addictive behaviors. We don't have to hide and cover up anymore because we are forgiven and alive in Christ. It is important to make the distinction between "having sin" and "being sin."

If we say we have no sin, we are _____.

What steps can you take to ensure that you are not going to be deceived any longer?

Read Romans 13:13,14.

What two things keep us from engaging in self-destructive behavior?

What do you think it means to clothe yourself with or put on the Lord Jesus Christ?

D. Stating the Truth ····················

The Truth:
The greatest commandment is to love the Lord my God will all my heart, soul and mind, and to love my neighbor as myself. I can do this because God first unconditionally loved and accepted me. By the grace of God I can conform to His image if I abide in Christ and live by the power of the Holy Spirit.

E. Illustrating the Truth ··············

Read page 178 in *Freedom from Addiction* beginning with "One of the greatest deceptions..." and ending with "...no matter how noble or spiritual." Then read pages 182-183 beginning with "The Stronghold of Insecurity" and ending with "...that's why relationships are so important." How do these illustrations relate to you?

F. Appropriating the Truth

List other lies that you have believed and the truth that you have learned.

The Lie That Binds You	The Truth That Sets You Free
I renounce the lie that:	I announce the truth that:
I will grow if I attend church and trust in their programs.	*I will grow if I know the truth and walk by faith.*
The goal of our instruction is knowledge.	*The goal of our instruction is love.*
I need to try harder to bear fruit.	*I need to abide in Christ and walk by the Spirit.*

G. Personalizing the Truth

Internalize the truth by personalizing Scripture and confessing it.

For example:
If I can preach like Paul and pray like Peter but don't have time for my family, I would be just as well off if I sang off-key in the church choir. If I know everything there is to know about everything, but don't have time for my children, I have missed the whole point of knowing anything. If I have faith to raise the dead, but don't show tangible love to my neighbor, I'm a big zero. If I am burned at the stake for preaching

the gospel, but don't have love, I have missed the whole meaning and purpose of life (from Corinthians 13:1-3).

Personalize any Scriptures that have been especially meaningful to you.

> An example from Matthew 22:37-40:
> I love the Lord with all my heart, with all my soul and with all my strength. This is the most important thing I do. In the same way I will love others as myself. This is the message of the whole Bible.

Are you now in the habit of renouncing the lies you have believed and announcing the truth?

Where Do We Go from Here?

If you did not precede this study with the books *Victory over the Darkness* and *The Bondage Breaker* and/or the video/audio series *Resolving Personal and Spiritual Conflicts*, we recommend that you do it now.

If you have completed that study, then we recommend that you go through *The Common Made Holy* by Dr. Neil T. Anderson and Dr. Robert Saucy. This book and study guide explain the whole process of sanctification. We also recommend that you use *Living Free in Christ* followed by *Daily in Christ* as daily devotionals.

Be sure to find a Christ-centered church that preaches the Word of

God, and don't be a spectator. Get involved in the life of the church and help others find their identity and freedom in Christ.

For further help and resources write or call:

Freedom in Christ Ministries
491 East Lambert Road
La Habra, CA 90631
(562) 691-9128

Mike and Julia Quarles
4590 Mountain Creek Dr.
Roswell, GA 30075
(770) 998-6487 (phone and fax)
102005.601@compuserve.com

The Overcomer's Covenant in Christ

1. I place all my trust and confidence in the Lord, and I put no confidence in the flesh. I declare myself to be dependent upon God. I know that I cannot save myself, nor set myself free by my own efforts and resources. I know that apart from Christ I can do nothing (see John 15:5). I know that all temptation is an attempt to get me to live my life independent from God, but God has provided a way of escape from sin (see 1 Corinthians 10:13).

2. I consciously and deliberately choose to submit to God and resist the devil by denying myself, picking up my cross daily and following Jesus. I know that my soul was never designed by God to function as master. I know that "rebellion is as the sin of witchcraft, and stubbornness is as iniquity and idolatry" (1 Samuel 15:23, *KJV*).

3. I choose to humble myself before the mighty hand of God in order that He may exalt me at the proper time. I know that God is opposed to the proud but gives grace to the humble (see James 4:6).

4. I declare the truth that I am dead to sin, freed from it and alive to God in Christ Jesus since I have died with Christ and was raised with Him. I know that the law and all my best efforts are unable to impart life, and that Jesus came to give me life.

5. I gladly embrace the truth that I am now a child of God who is unconditionally loved and accepted. I reject the lie that I have to perform to be accepted. I also reject my fallen and natural identity which was derived from the world. I know that it is not what I do that determines who I am, but who I am that determines what I do.

6. I declare that sin shall no longer be master over me because I am not under the law, but under grace and there is no more guilt or condemnation because I am spiritually alive in Christ Jesus. I am a servant of a new covenant, not of the letter, but of the Spirit; for the letter kills, but the Spirit gives life.

7. I renounce every unrighteous use of my body and I commit myself to no longer be conformed to this world, but rather to be transformed by the renewing of my mind. I choose to believe the truth and walk in it regardless of my feelings or circumstances. I

know that before I came to Christ my mind was programmed according to this world and I used my body as an instrument of unrighteousness, thereby allowing sin to reign in my mortal body (see Romans 6:12,13).

8. I commit myself to take every thought captive to the obedience of Christ, and choose to think upon that which is true, honorable, right, pure and lovely. I know that the Holy Spirit explicitly says that in later times some will fall away from the faith, paying attention to deceitful spirits and doctrines, or teachings of demons (see 1 Timothy 4:1).

9. I commit myself to God's great goal for my life to conform to His image. I know that I will face many trials, but God has given me the victory and I am not a victim, but an overcomer in Christ. The grace of God will enable me to triumph over every trial resulting in proven character.

10. I choose to adopt the attitude of Christ which is to do nothing from selfishness or empty conceit, but with humility of mind I will regard others as more important than myself; and not merely look out for my own personal interests, but also the interests of others (see Philippians 2:3-5). I know that "'It is more blessed to give than to receive'" (Acts 20:35).

The following page is intended for your use. It can be taken out and placed in your Bible or in a prominent place to remind you of your covenant in Christ and who you are in Christ.

The Overcomer's Covenant in Christ

Abridged Version

1. I place all my trust and confidence in the Lord and I put no confidence in the flesh. I declare myself to be dependent upon God.

2. I consciously and deliberately choose to submit to God and resist the devil by denying myself, picking up my cross daily and following Jesus.

3. I choose to humble myself before the mighty hand of God in order that He may exalt me at the proper time.

4. I declare the truth that I am dead to sin, freed from it and alive to God in Christ Jesus since I have died with Christ and was raised with Him.

5. I gladly embrace the truth that I am now a child of God who is unconditionally loved and accepted.

6. I declare that sin shall no longer be master over me because I am not under the law but under grace, and there is no more guilt or condemnation because I am spiritually alive in Christ Jesus.

7. I renounce every unrighteous use of my body and I commit myself to no longer be conformed to this world, but rather be transformed by the renewing of my mind. I choose to believe the truth and walk in it, regardless of my feelings or circumstances.

8. I commit myself to take every thought captive to the obedience of Christ, and choose to think upon that which is true, honorable, right, pure and lovely.

9. I commit myself to God's great goal for my life to conform to His image.

10. I choose to adopt the attitude of Christ which has nothing to do with selfishness or empty conceit, but with humility of mind I will regard others as more important than myself; and not merely look out for my own personal interests, but also the interests of others.

Who I Am in Christ

I Am Accepted

John 1:12	I am God's child.
John 15:15	I am Christ's friend.
Romans 5:1	I have been justified.
1 Corinthians 6:17	I am united with the Lord and one with Him in spirit.
1 Corinthians 6:20	I have been bought with a price—I belong to God.
1 Corinthians 12:27	I am a member of Christ's body.
Ephesians 1:1	I am a saint.
Ephesians 1:5	I have been adopted as God's child.
Ephesians 2:18	I have direct access to God through the Holy Spirit.
Colossians 1:14	I have been redeemed and forgiven of all my sins.
Colossians 2:10	I am complete in Christ.

I Am Secure

Romans 8:1,2	I am free from condemnation.
Romans 8:28	I am assured that all things work together for good.
Romans 8:31ff	I am free from any condemning charges against me.
Romans 8:35ff	I cannot be separated from the love of God.
2 Corinthians 1:21	I have been established, anointed and sealed by God.
Colossians 3:3	I am hidden with Christ in God.
Philippians 1:6	I am confident that the good work that God has begun in me will be perfected.
Philippians 3:20	I am a citizen of heaven.
2 Timothy 1:7	I have not been given a spirit of fear, but of power, love and a sound mind.
Hebrews 4:16	I can find grace and mercy in time of need.
1 John 5:18	I am born of God and the evil one cannot touch me.

I Am Significant

Matthew 5:13	I am the salt and light of the earth.
John 15:1,5	I am a branch of the true vine, a channel of His life.
John 15:16	I have been chosen and appointed to bear fruit.
Acts 1:8	I am Christ's personal witness.
1 Corinthians 3:16	I am God's temple.
2 Corinthians 5:17ff	I am a minister of reconciliation.
2 Corinthians 6:1	I am God's coworker.
Ephesians 2:6	I am seated with Christ in the heavenly realm.
Ephesians 2:10	I am God's workmanship.
Ephesians 3:12	I may approach God with freedom and confidence.
Philippians 4:13	I can do all things through Christ who strengthens me.

Freedom in Christ Resources

Parenting Resources

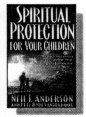

Spiritual Protection for Your Children
by Neil Anderson and Peter and Sue Vanderhook

The fascinating true story of an average middle-class American family's spiritual battle on the home front and the lessons we can all learn about protecting our families from the enemy's attacks. Includes helpful prayers for children of various ages.

Hardcover $19 • 300 pp. B021

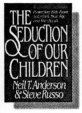

The Seduction of Our Children
by Neil Anderson and Steve Russo

A battle is raging for the minds of our children. It's a battle parents <u>must</u> win. This timely book will prepare parents to counter the world's assault against their families. Includes helpful prayers for children of various ages.

Paper $9 • 245 pp. B004

The Seduction of Our Children Video
by Neil Anderson

This parenting series will change the way you view the spiritual development of your children. Helpful insights are offered on many parenting issues, such as discipline, communication and spiritual oversight of children. A panel of experts share their advice.

Video Tape Set $85 • 6 lessons V002   Audio Tape Set $35 • 6 lessons A002
Additional workbooks $4 • 49 pp. W002

Youth Resources

Stomping Out the Darkness
by Neil Anderson and Dave Park

This youth version of *Victory Over the Darkness* shows youth how to break free and discover the joy of their identity in Christ (Part 1 of 2).

Paper $9 • 210 pp. B101   Study Guide Paper $8 • 137 pp. G101

The Bondage Breaker Youth Edition
by Neil Anderson and Dave Park

This youth best-seller shares the process of breaking bondages and the *Youth Steps to Freedom in Christ*. Read this with *Stomping Out the Darkness* (Part 2 of 2).

Paper $8 • 227 pp. B102   Study Guide Paper $6 • 128 pp. G102

Busting Free!
by Neil Anderson and Dave Park

This is a dynamic Group Study of *Stomping Out the Darkness* and *The Bondage Breaker Youth Edition*. It has complete teaching notes for a 13 week (or 26 week) Bible study with reproducible handouts. Ideal for Sunday school classes, Bible studies and youth discipleship groups of all kinds.

Paper $17 • 163 pp. G103

Youth Topics

Helping Young People Find Freedom in Christ
by Neil Anderson and Rich Miller

This youth version provides comprehensive, hands-on biblical discipleship counseling training for parents, youth workers and youth pastors, equipping them to help young people. This resource is Part 3 continuing from the message of Parts 1 and 2.

Paper $13 • 300 pp. B112

Know Light, No Fear
by Neil Anderson and Rich Miller

In this youth version of *Walking in the Light* young people learn how to know God's will for their lives. They will discover key truths about divine guidance and helpful warnings for avoiding spiritual counterfeits.

Paper $10 • 250 pp. B111

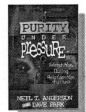

Purity Under Pressure
by Neil Anderson and Dave Park

Real answers for real world pressures! Youth will find out the difference between being friends, dating and having a relationship. No hype, no big lectures; just straightforward talk about living free in Christ.

Paper $8 • 200 pp. B104

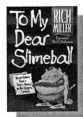

To My Dear Slimeball
by Rich Miller

In the spirit of C. S. Lewis' *Screwtape Letters*, this humorous story, filled with biblical truth, is an allegory of the spiritual battle every believer faces. Discover how 15-year-old David's life is amazingly similar to your own.

Paper $8 each • 250 pp. B103

Youth Devotionals

These four 40-day devotionals help young people understand God's love and their identity in Christ. Teens will learn to establish a positive spiritual habit of getting into God's Word on a daily basis.

Extreme Faith
Paper $8
204 pp. B106

Reality Check
Paper $8
200 pp. B107

Awesome God
Paper $8
200 pp. B108

Ultimate Love
Paper $8
200 pp. B109

Freedom in Christ Resources

Helping Others Find Freedom in Christ

by Neil Anderson

This book provides comprehensive, hands-on biblical discipleship counseling training for lay leaders, counselors and pastors, equipping them to help others. This resource is Part 3, continuing from the message of Parts 1 and 2.

Hard $17 • 297 pp. B016   Paper $12 • 297 pp. B015

Helping Others Find Freedom in Christ Training Manual and Study Guide

by Neil Anderson and Tom McGee

This companion to *Helping Others Find Freedom in Christ* provides leadership training and a step-by-step plan to establish a freedom ministry (Discipleship Counseling ministry) in your church or organization.

Paper $12 • 229 pp. G015

Helping Others Find Freedom in Christ Video Training Program

This Video Training Program is a complete training kit for churches and groups who want to establish a freedom ministry using the *Steps to Freedom in Christ*. Includes four 45-minute video lessons, a *Helping Others Find Freedom in Christ* book, a *Training Manual/Study Guide* and six *Steps to Freedom in Christ* guidebooks.

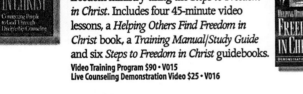

Video Training Program $90 • V015
Live Counseling Demonstration Video $25 • V016

Released From Bondage

by Neil Anderson

This book shares true stories of freedom from obsessive thoughts, compulsive behaviors, guilt, satanic ritual abuse, childhood abuse and demonic strongholds, combined with helpful commentary from Dr. Anderson.

Paper $13 • 258 pp. B006

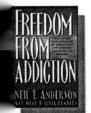

Freedom From Addiction

by Neil Anderson and Mike and Julia Quarles

A book like no other on true recovery! This unique Christ-centered model has helped thousands break free from alcoholism, drug addiction and other addictive behaviors. The Quarles' amazing story will encourage every reader!

Hard $19 • 356 pp. B018   Paper $13 • 356 pp. B019
Video Study $90 • V019

Spiritual Conflicts and Counseling

by Neil Anderson

This series presents advanced counseling insights and practical, biblical answers to help others find their freedom in Christ. It is the full content from Dr. Anderson's advanced seminar of the same name.

Video Tape Set $95 • 8 lessons V003   Audio Tape Set $40 • 8 lessons A003
Additional Workbooks $8 • Paper 53 pp. W003

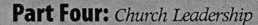

Setting Your Church Free

by Neil Anderson and Charles Mylander

This powerful book reveals how pastors and church leaders can lead their entire churches to freedom by discovering the key issues of both corporate bondage and corporate freedom. A must-read for every church leader.

Hard $17 • 352 pp. B012   Paper $12 • 352 pp. B013

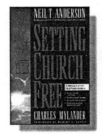

Setting Your Church Free Video

by Neil Anderson and Charles Mylander

This leadership series presents the powerful principles taught in *Setting Your Church Free*. Ideal for church staffs and boards to study and discuss together. The series ends with the *Steps to Setting Your Church Free*.

Video Tape Set $95 • 8 lessons V006   Audio Tape Set $40 • 8 lessons A006
Additional workbooks $6 • paper 42 pp. W006

Topical Resources

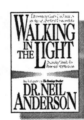

Walking in the Light

by Neil Anderson

Everyone wants to know God's will for their life. Dr. Anderson explains the fascinating spiritual dimensions of divine guidance and how to avoid spiritual counterfeits. Includes a personal application guide for each chapter.

Paper $13 • 234 pp. B011

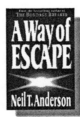

A Way of Escape

by Neil Anderson

Talking about sex is never easy. This vital book provides real answers for sexual struggles, unwanted thoughts, compulsive habits or a painful past. Don't learn to just cope, learn how to resolve your sexual issues in Christ.

Paper $10 • 238 pp. B014

The Common Made Holy

by Neil Anderson and Robert Saucy

An extraordinary book on how Christ transforms the life of a believer. Dr. Anderson and Dr. Saucy provide answers to help resolve the confusion about our "perfect" identity in Christ in our "imperfect" world.

Hard $17 • 375 pp. B017
Study Guide $8 • G017

The Christ Centered Marriage

by Neil Anderson and Charles Mylander

Husbands and wives, discover and enjoy your freedom in Christ together! Break free from old habit patterns and enjoy greater intimacy, joy and fulfillment.

Hard $19 • 300 pp. B020   Marriage Steps $6 • 36 pp. G020
Video Seminar $90 • V020

Freedom in Christ Resources

| Part One: *Resolving Personal Conflicts* | Part Two: *Resolving Spiritual Conflicts* |

Part One: *Resolving Personal Conflicts*

Victory Over the Darkness
by Neil Anderson

Start here! This best-seller combined with *The Bondage Breaker* will show you how to find your freedom in Christ. Realize the power of your identity in Christ!

Paper $10 • 245 pp. B001
Study Guide • Paper $9 • 139 pp. G001

Living Free in Christ
by Neil Anderson

Based on the inspirational "Who Am I?" list from *Victory Over the Darkness*, here are 36 powerful chapters and prayers that will transform your life and dramatically show how Christ meets all of your deepest needs!

Paper $13 • 310 pp. B008
Free in Christ Audio $10 • A030

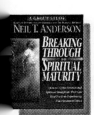

Daily in Christ
by Neil and Joanne Anderson

This uplifting 365 day devotional will encourage, motivate and challenge you to live daily in Christ. There's a one-page devotional and brief heart-felt prayer for each day. Celebrate and experience your freedom all year.

Hard $17 • 365 pp. B010

Breaking Through to Spiritual Maturity
by Neil Anderson

This is a dynamic Group Study of *Victory Over the Darkness* and *The Bondage Breaker*. Complete with teaching notes for a 13 week (or 26 week) Bible study, with reproducible handouts. Ideal for Sunday school classes, Bible studies, and discipleship groups.

Paper $17 • 151 pp. G003

Resolving Personal Conflicts
by Neil Anderson

This series covers the first half of Dr. Anderson's exciting conference. Learn the truth about who you are in Christ, how to renew your mind, heal damaged emotions and truly forgive others (Part 1 of a 2-part series).

Video Tape Set $95 • 8 lessons V001
Audio Tape Set $40 • 8 lessons A001
Additional workbooks $5 • Paper 32 pp. W001

Resolving Spiritual Conflicts & Cross-Cultural Ministry
by Dr. Timothy Warner

This series has powerful lessons on missions, world view and warfare relationships that are extremely helpful for every Christian. It provides key insights for spiritual growth and ministry.

Video Tape Set $85 • 8 lessons V005
Audio Tape Set $35 • 8 lessons A005
Additional workbooks $8 • paper 47 pp. W005

Part Two: *Resolving Spiritual Conflicts*

The Bondage Breaker
by Neil Anderson

This best-seller shares the definitive process of breaking bondages and the *Steps to Freedom in Christ*. Read this with *Victory Over the Darkness* and you will be able to resolve your personal and spiritual conflicts.

Paper $10 • 247 pp. B002   Study Guide • Paper $6 • 121 pp. G002

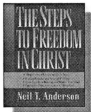

The Steps to Freedom in Christ
by Neil Anderson

This is a handy version of the *Steps to Freedom in Christ*, the discipleship counseling process from *The Bondage Breaker*. It is ideal for personal use or for helping another person who wants to find his freedom.

Paper $2 • 19 pp. G004

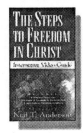

The Steps to Freedom in Christ Video
with Neil Anderson

In this special video experience, Dr. Neil Anderson personally leads you or a loved one through the bondage-breaking Steps to Freedom in Christ in the privacy of your living room. Includes *The Steps to Freedom in Christ* booklet.

Video $20 • 70 minutes • V010

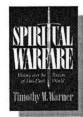

Spiritual Warfare
by Dr. Timothy Warner

This concise book offers balanced, biblical insights on spiritual warfare with practical information and ammunition for winning the spiritual battle. Every reader will benefit by learning from the author's extensive experience.

Paper $9 • 160 pp. B007

Resolving Spiritual Conflicts
by Neil Anderson

This series offers the second half of Dr. Anderson's exciting conference. Every believer needs to fully understand his position, authority and protection in Christ, and the enemy's tactics (Part 2 of a 2-part series).

Video Tape Set $95 • 8 lessons V002   Audio Tape Set $40 • 8 lessons A002
Additional workbooks $6 • Paper 49 pp. W002

Available at your local Christian bookstore or from
Freedom in Christ
491 E. Lambert Road
La Habra, CA 90631-6136

Phone: (562) 691-9128 Fax (562) 691-4035
Internet: www.freedominchrist.com
Email: 73430.2630@compuserve.com

How Freedom in Christ Resources Work Together

This chart shows "at a glance" how Freedom in Christ's resources AND conferences interrelate and their correct order of progression from basic to advanced.

Part One

THIS IS FREEDOM IN CHRIST'S CORE MESSAGE OF RESOLVING PERSONAL AND SPIRITUAL CONFLICTS

- Victory Over the Darkness
- Victory Over the Darkness Study Guide
- Living Free in Christ
- Daily in Christ
- The Bondage Breaker
- The Bondage Breaker Study Guide
- Steps to Freedom in Christ
- Spiritual Warfare
- Breaking Through to Spiritual Maturity Teaching Guide
  (Covers Parts 1 and 2)

"Resolving Personal Conflicts" and "Resolving Spiritual Conflicts" Conference and Audios/Videos
(Covers Parts 1 and 2)

"Free in Christ" Audio and "Steps to Freedom in Christ" Video

"Resolving Spiritual Conflicts and Cross-cultural Ministry" Conference and Audios/Videos
(Covers Parts 1 and 2)

"Shepherd's Time Out" Conference
(Covers Parts 1, 2 and 3)

"If you hold to My teaching, you are really My disciples. Then you will know the truth, and the truth will set you free."

*See separate list for youth or young adult resources!

Part Two

Part Three

PRACTICAL BIBLICAL ANSWERS FOR DISCIPLESHIP COUNSELING

- Helping Others Find Freedom in Christ
- Helping Others Find Freedom in Christ Training Manual and Study Guide
- Released From Bondage
- Freedom From Addiction

"Spiritual Conflicts and Counseling" Audios/Videos

"Helping Others Find Freedom in Christ" Video Training Program

"Helping Others Find Freedom in Christ" Counseling Demonstration Video

"Church Leadership and Discipleship Counseling" Conference

"Freedom From Addiction" Conference and Video Study

Part Four

CHURCH LEADERSHIP

- Setting Your Church Free
- Steps to Setting Your Church Free

"Setting Your Church Free" Conference and Audios/Videos

Topical

- Walking in the Light
- A Way of Escape
- The Common Made Holy
- The Common Made Holy Study Guide
- The Christ-Centered Marriage
  (3 versions of the marriage Steps)
- Spiritual Protection for Your Children
- The Seduction of Our Children
- Rivers of Revival

"The Christ-Centered Marriage" Conference and Video Seminar

"The Seduction of Our Children" Conference and Audios/Videos

Contact Freedom in Christ at:

491 E. Lambert Road
La Habra, CA 90631-6136
Phone: (562) 691-9128
Fax (562) 691-4035

World Wide Web:
www.freedominchrist.com

Email:
73430.2630@compuserve.com

You've Seen the Video. Now Read the Book.

As you lead your **Freedom from Addiction** group, photocopy these coupons and give them to each person attending. The coupons are good for $2.00 off each purchase of the **Freedom from Addiction** paperback book and the **Freedom from Addiction Workbook**.

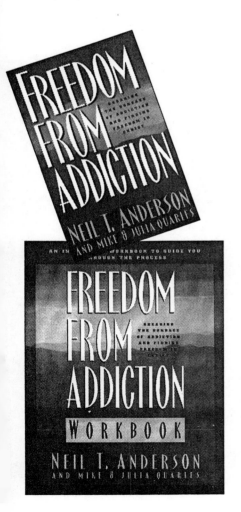

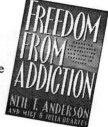